Finding JOY in Cancer

DENNIS DOCHEFF, ED.D.

ISBN 979-8-88832-839-2 (paperback)
ISBN 979-8-88832-840-8 (digital)

Christian Faith Publishing
832 Park Avenue
Meadville, PA 16335
www.christianfaithpublishing.com

Printed in the United States of America

Consider it pure joy, my brothers and
sisters, whenever you face trials of many
kinds, because you know that the testing
of your faith produces perseverance.

—James 1:2–3 NIV

Contents

Acknowledgments

Typically, authors include acknowledgments at the conclusion of their books. In this case, I chose to acknowledge those who have provided significant inspiration in my life before the book begins. They are more important than my story.

First, I recognize the Lord of my life. God has blessed me with so much. He loves me, He cares for me, He guides me, He carries me when I need Him, He gives me strength when I sometimes falter, and He forgives me of my sin (which I do daily). Thank You, Lord, for the gift of eternal life!

I must share admiration for my wife, Keri, who has supported all the endeavors throughout my life and career once she joined me on this wild ride. Every day she makes me feel like I own the world. Her kind, gentle ways touch my heart every single day. When I was deathly ill, she was my main caregiver. She saw me through leukemia and, about fourteen years later, throat cancer. I'd say I consider myself the luckiest guy on the face of the earth (thanks, Lou Gehrig), but luck had nothing to do with it. Keri is a gift from God. Thanks for marrying me, Keri!

Much appreciation to my kids—Dodge, Payton, and Emily. Over the years, they have provided me with such great pleasure, such JOY! Each one is unique and special in their own way. I am so proud of the quality people they have shown themselves to be. I pray for each of them every day, asking for safety and guidance from God. I hope that they can maintain a strong relationship with God as He will be a light unto their paths.

Boundless gratitude to those doctors, nurses, technicians, and others who saved my life. They perform miracles every day. I am just lucky to be one of the many who benefited from their knowledge, expertise, and caregiving ways.

I am thankful for the many special friends and professional colleagues who have supported me over the years. I worked to earn their respect; but their kindness, care, and love overwhelmed me during the difficult times of my infirmity. I cannot list names out of fear of omitting someone. Let's just say that my friends know who they are.

> *For God so loved the world that he gave his one and only Son, that whoever believes in him shall not perish but have eternal life. For God did not send his Son into the world to condemn the world, but to save the world through him. Whoever believes in him is not condemned, but whoever does not believe stands condemned already because they have not believed in the name of God's one and only Son.*
> (John 3:16–18)

> *Surrounded by Your glory*
> *What will my heart feel?*
> *Will I dance for You Jesus*
> *Or in awe of You be still?*
> *Will I stand in Your presence*
> *Or to my knees, will I fall?*
> *Will I sing hallelujah?*
> *Will I be able to speak at all?*
> *I can only imagine*
> *I can only imagine.*
> (Bart Millard, "I Can Only Imagine")

Opening Prayer

Lord, thank You for being who You are—the Creator of the entire universe. Thank You for Your love, grace, and mercy. Thank You for the gift of eternal life through Your Son, Jesus. Thank You for the blessings and promises You give to encourage and support my walk with You. Thank You for forgiving me of my sins. Thank You for walking alongside me when I am strong and carrying me when I am weak. Thank You for the gift and trial of my cancer, through which You drew me nearer to You—JOY! Help me be the person You aim for me to be. Please help me stay on Your path for me, trusting You along the way, having faith in Your will for me. I pray that this little book might give others encouragement and hope when facing difficult times. Thank You for the JOY of knowing You. In Your Son's name, I pray. Amen.

> *May the God of hope fill you with all JOY and peace as you trust in him, so that you may overflow with hope by the power of the Holy Spirit.* (Romans 15:13; emphasis added)

> *[A]nd though you have not seen Him, you love Him, and though you do not see Him now, but believe in Him, you greatly rejoice with JOY inexpressible and full of glory, obtaining as the outcome of your faith the salvation of your souls.* (1 Peter 1:8–9; emphasis added)

Introduction

The year 1955—it was a very good year! Quite a bit happened in 1955. The polio vaccine, created by Jonas Salk, was affirmed to be safe and effective; Rosa Parks was arrested for not giving up her seat on a bus to a White passenger; the United States began its involvement in the Vietnam War; Disneyland opened in Southern California; and *The Mickey Mouse Club* debuted on ABC. In addition, Albert Einstein, James Dean, Cy Young, and Dale Carnegie died that year.

In America, the average annual wage was $3,851; the average monthly rent was $87; the average cost of a new car was $1,900; the average cost of a gallon of gas was 23¢; and the minimum wage was raised to $1 per hour. The first McDonald's east of the Mississippi River opened in 1955, and Coca-Cola was sold in cans for the first time (prior to this year, Coca-Cola had only been sold in glass bottles). The top songs for the year were the following: (1) "Cherry Pink and Apple Blossom White" (by Perez Prado), (2) "Rock Around the Clock" (by Bill Haley and the Comets), and (3) "The Yellow Rose of Texas" (by Mitch Miller). The Brooklyn Dodgers won the World Series. And, oh yeah…I was born in 1955.

I was the third son in a family of five—yes, the baby of the family. As I grew up in Southern California, it is now hard to believe that our family of five had only one car, shared only one bathroom, and had just one phone that was attached to the wall. How did we do it? I was a happy kid. A rough-and-tumble kid, I loved to play…hard. I loved school. I loved the teachers, the other students, and my friends. Life was pretty great! In fourth grade, I had my first PE teacher, Mr. Roy Swett. Yes, that was his real name. If only it had been spelled *Sweat*, how great would that have been? That year, I received the Most Valuable Player Award of the after-school flag football program (I still have the certificate to prove it). In the spring of that year, our family also moved up north to the San Francisco Bay Area.

In 1968, I accepted Jesus Christ as my personal Savior. I loved going to children's church and competing with a girl, Terri, to memorize the most Bible verses. One Sunday evening, my oldest brother wanted to head home after youth group, but I really wanted to stay for the service. I didn't know why, but I just felt the need to stay. At the conclusion of the service, I found myself walking forward to profess my faith. Although I understood the overall story of Jesus back then, I am pretty sure I didn't really fully understand what it meant. That is true for many people; as we mature in faith, we understand our salvation more and appreciate it more. To me, the trick is to have an ongoing maturity in our love for and study of Christ while not losing that childlike innocent "wow factor" of knowing Jesus.

Later that year, my mom and dad split up. Neither Mom nor Dad continued to go to church, so my churchgoing days ended as well. Mom, one of my brothers (Tim), and I moved into an apartment. But after one year, Tim went off to college, so it was just me and Mom. I finished high school in 1974. My high school experience was filled with sports (football, basketball, and track) and numerous choral groups (Concert Choir, Men's Ensemble, and Madrigals). It seemed I was either in the locker room or the choir room.

I loved hanging out in the choir room. In Concert Choir, every Friday, Mr. Smith (yes, that was his real name) had all the students sit "co-ed"—boy, girl, boy, girl—instead of in choral parts (altos, tenors, etc.). After going co-ed, we would all face to the right and give back rubs. Then we'd face to the left and give back rubs. That didn't happen in the locker room! At the conclusion of the class period, we would sing "The Lord Bless You and Keep You."

The Lord bless you and keep you,
The Lord lift His countenance upon you.
And give you peace, and give you peace,
The Lord make His face to shine upon you.
And be gracious unto you, and be gracious,
The Lord be gracious, gracious unto you.
Amen, amen, amen.
Amen, amen, amen.
(John Rutter, "The Lord Bless You and Keep You")

Wow! What a way to end the week! The Biblical reference for the song is Numbers 6:24–26. Hearing this song brings back nothing but fond memories.

Then off to college I went. I attended a small college in Spokane, Washington, played football for two years, and was on the track-and-field team for four years. At the end of four years, I was an elementary school teacher and a sport coach (football, basketball, and track). I ended up teaching numerous subjects at a variety of grade levels over the years. I completed my master's degree and my doctorate and ended up teaching at the university level. I was married when I was thirty-three years of age, and my wife and I raised three wonderful children.

If I had to select a theme song that described how I look at life, it would be a song sung by Neil Diamond, "I Am… I Said." In this song, there are lyrics that sum up how I feel about my life:

Did you ever read about a frog
Who dreamed of bein' a king
And then became one?
Well except for the names
And a few other changes
If you talk about me
The story is the same one.

I was healthy and happy most of my life. As I recall, I missed only four and a half days of school because of illness during my first ten years of teaching. All was good.

Fast forward about twenty-five years. I was married, with three children, and teaching at a university. I was becoming stronger in my faith and growing nearer to God. Life was grand. I truly was a frog who had dreamed of becoming a king and then became one. Then one day, following a doctor's appointment, my wife and I were driving to the pharmacy to fill a prescription. We received a phone call. The conversation went something like this:

"Hello."

"Hi. Is this Dennis?"

"Yes, it is."

"This is the doctor's office. What are you doing right now?"

"I am driving to the pharmacy."

"The doctor wants you to go to the emergency room right now."

"Why?"

"Your white blood cell count is nearly zero. You need to get their now!"

So we went to the emergency room. They were waiting for me and immediately told me to put on a mask (this was prepandemic). They took me into a room and ran some tests. Bottom line: I was diagnosed with leukemia. My initial reaction when the doctor told me was "What do we need to do now?" Ever since that day, I seemed to always be sick, but we beat it! About fourteen years later, cancer stuck its nose into my life. It was cancer of the throat. I was older and more mature in my faith and decided to face cancer with the Lord by my side. He was with me throughout my leukemia years, but I wasn't as clear about His presence as I was when the throat cancer diagnosis was made. I knew I needed Him to help me through this adversity.

Thinking like a coach, I knew I needed a game plan. I decided that for me to survive this fight with throat cancer, it would require me to have a focused approach with God in the forefront. I had always liked and appreciated James 1:2–3:

> *Consider it pure JOY, my brothers and sisters, when-*
> *ever you face trials of many kinds, because you know*
> *that the testing of your faith produces perseverance.*

But I didn't really grasp its true meaning. WAIT! What? Cancer ain't no gift! Cancer is evil. Cancer is pain. Cancer causes families to experience sorrow. Cancer is scary. Cancer is a foreign body that can attack a person at his or her core. Cancer causes the shutting down of our bodies' organs, blood vessels, nerves, and more. Cancer causes severe weight loss—unhealthy weight loss. Cancer causes fatigue, the kind of fatigue that makes getting out of bed a chore. Cancer saps people of all their energy. Cancer is death!

Cancer sometimes makes people question whether God loves them. Cancer causes some people to lose their faith. They think, *Why me, God?* and drift away from Him. How was I going to find JOY in cancer? I wanted to have a positive attitude toward my treatment, and I needed God to get me through it. I decided to make that bit of Scripture from the book of James the focus of my fight against cancer. Somehow God grabbed my heart and, in essence, said, "Come along with me, son." I was determined to somehow find JOY in this killer.

So we fought it. We beat it. And I did find JOY throughout the entire cancer experience. That inspired me to share my story with others. It began with a presentation at my church on a Wednesday night, titled "Finding the JOY in Cancer." My talk was fairly well received. Then this thought came to me: *Maybe my story could positively impact others if I shared my search for JOY by writing a book.* That's how this document came about. My purpose is to communicate my experiences, impressions, fears, and triumphs to share how God took a hold of me and practically carried me through my treatment and recovery.

Prior to reading my little book, readers are encouraged to begin with prayer. A simple prayer will do, perhaps something like "Dear Lord, let the words in this book help me draw nearer to You. Help me understand how I might find JOY in all things every moment of every day. In Jesus's name I pray. Amen." This book chronicles the events that span approximately one year, from cancer diagnosis to treatment to recovery. Throughout the book, I share plenty of stories from my life and some meaningful quotes. Also included are selected Bible verses, all of which can be found in the New International

Version. In addition, each chapter ends with a Scripture passage and a portion of a worship song. That may allow the reader to stop and worship for a brief moment. Before you turn the pages to begin chapter 1, please permit me to share my encouragement and enthusiasm with the reader. It is hoped that this short book will allow the reader to think about how he or she might find JOY when encountering trials and adversity.

> *The LORD is my shepherd, I lack nothing. He makes me lie down in green pastures, he leads me beside quiet waters, he refreshes my soul. He guides me along the right paths for his name's sake. Even though I walk through the darkest valley, I will fear no evil, for you are with me, your rod and your staff, they comfort me. You prepare a table before me in the presence of my enemies. You anoint my head with oil; my cup overflows. Surely your goodness and love will follow me all the days of my life, and I will dwell in the house of the LORD forever.* (Psalm 23)

I bring an offering of
Worship to my King.
No one on earth deserves
The praises that I sing.
Jesus, may You receive
The honor that You're due;
O Lord, I bring an offering to You.
(Paul Baloche, "Offering")

CHAPTER I

Happy Thanksgiving

Thanksgiving—what a great time of the year! For many, it is a holiday that celebrates family and the love shared within an entire clan of family members. Families get together, sometimes traveling many miles, to spend quality time together and eat great food. They also reminisce about the old times, talk about the present, and sometimes share thoughts about the future. The holiday is likewise about spending time with friends. Whether meeting up with friends at church, in the workplace, in the neighborhood, or any other place, seeing friends at Thanksgiving time seems extra special. Regardless of who a person is with, Thanksgiving is a time of sharing love with others.

I remember Thanksgiving when I was a youngster. Sometimes we would go to one of the grandmas' houses. As soon as we arrived, one could not help but notice the aroma that permeated the house. One of my grandmas always had Ovaltine. That was always a treat! At the other grandma's house, she always had root beer. It was the best! The food smelled so good; it probably tasted good too. There were times when I couldn't be sure how good the food tasted because the choice morsels that were cooked for hours were wolfed down so quickly. Also, I wouldn't touch most of the food provided as I was quite a picky eater. If it was green, it didn't make it onto my plate; my dish was filled with only turkey and mashed potatoes, both covered with gravy. Of course, there was an endless supply of rolls that were to be used to sop up more gravy. Forget the cranberry sauce, forget the three-bean salad (actually, you can forget any kind of salad), forget the yams (gross), and forget anything else on the table. Turkey, mashed potatoes, rolls, and gravy—it was great!

There were some years where we visited friends. When we arrived, us kids would almost immediately head for the backyard to play football. Our family had three boys, one set of friends had two boys, another set of friends had two boys, and another family had three boys and two girls. The girls didn't play. But whichever friends were there, we all played football. Being one of the younger kids, I was not the best player, but it didn't really matter. It was fun just to play. Spending the holiday with friends seemed to create stronger ties; friends became *good friends*, people you could rely on. The playtime was great. When we weren't playing football, we were watching football games on the television set. And then we would eat and eat and eat some more! Of course, the menu for me never changed.

When I was grown up enough to live on my own, Thanksgiving was quite a bit different. The menu changed because I was not going to attempt to cook a turkey for one person. So the Thanksgiving turkey was replaced with turkey hot dogs—eight of them. No mashed potatoes; they were replaced with a bag of chips, potato chips. And, of course, there was the obligatory two-liter bottle of soda pop. Note: It goes without saying that the TV was on all day—football! So this was how the day played out: During halftime of the first football game, the Thanksgiving feast began. Four hotdogs were boiled and then placed between two slices of bread, with ketchup. Yes, a turkey hot dog sandwich! Usually, a half bag of chips was consumed with the dogs. Everything was washed down with the soda pop, typically some kind of diet cola. I preferred Diet Coke, but since I was always a thrifty shopper, the cheapest brand of diet cola was part of the menu even if it didn't taste as good as Diet Coke. Once this fine banquet was wolfed down, it was usually time for the second half of the game to begin. By the time the first football game was over and the halftime of the second game arrived, it was time to eat again. So another four–hot dog sandwich, the rest of the chips, and most of the pop was devoured. It was me, the TV, and the feast!

All families are different. Some families openly share love for one another, while other families are a bit more reserved with their feelings. At holiday time, we participated in the "family thing," but there was not a lot of love shared openly in our family. I don't recall being told "I love you" by my parents as a kid. Even when we were grown, it was rarely heard from Mom or Dad. That is probably why my best role models growing up were my teachers and coaches. They taught me so much. They also demonstrated their care and concern for me. Now I know my parents cared for me; they just weren't very demonstrative about it. Later in life, I found role models in professional colleagues and people from church.

Allow me to share a couple of Thanksgiving Day stories in my life. The first story is from when I was in my late twenties. I was an elementary school (grades K–8) principal in one building and an assistant principal and junior high athletic director in another school building. I was also the head high school football coach and the head high school girls' basketball coach. On this Thanksgiving, I was enjoying my usual football on TV and Thanksgiving hot dog feast when I received a telephone call from my dad. He said, "Happy Thanksgiving," and I reciprocated. Then he proceeded to tell me that I was being taken out of his will. He explained that it was a compliment to me. He said that my oldest brother had two kids and that my other brother always seemed to be in some kind of need. "If something happens to me, they both could probably use an inheritance," he explained. "I don't need to worry about you. You'll always be okay." So I guess it was a compliment. It just didn't feel like it. The phone conversation was soon over, and I went back to my TV football and hot dog feast. Happy Thanksgiving!

My second Thanksgiving Day story took place in 1988. I was thirty-two years old and once again having my typical Thanksgiving feast, but I was feeling a bit down. I have never been depressed in life. Actually, I usually have quite a positive, upbeat approach to life. But on this day, I was pretty low. I was tired of being alone. I wanted someone in my life, someone who I could love and receive love from in return. I did something I had not done for quite a while: I prayed. I asked God to bring someone into my life. I wanted a life partner. I wanted a family. Now I didn't expect to pray and then hear a knock at my door ten minutes later, with the girl of my dreams standing on my doorstep, waiting for me. However, right after the new year began—actually, it was on January 8—I met someone that would eventually become my wife.

On that first day of the university semester, Keri Nelsen walked into my classroom. It was a health and PE class for future elementary teachers. It didn't take long for me to become interested in this nice, cute young lady. Maybe it was the way she loped across my gym, maybe it was her kind and gentle demeanor, or maybe she was the answer to my prayer and a gift from God. Toward the end of the semester, we would meet up in the fitness center and work out together. At the end of the workout, we would sit and stretch…and talk. When the semester ended and she was no longer in my class, we went on a date. It was immediate. At the beginning of April, I asked her to marry me, and she said yes! Later that August, we were married. At the time of this writing, we have been happily married thirty-three and a half years and yet to have an argument. Clearly, God made this happen.

This brings us to the present day. Now that I am married, we have our own family routines; I am able to sit back and watch the football games on TV from the recliner while my wife, Keri, creates more food than our family can consume. The smells fill the house, and a variety of bags of chips are opened to enhance the football-watching experience. Our kids are grown, so we typically watch the games together. When they were younger, we might play board games or some kind of card game (while the football was on the tube in the background). Spending time together was great for our family. One unwritten rule was that the Thanksgiving meal had to coincide with halftime of one of the football games. After all, I was a football coach; it just seemed right.

In the fall of 2021, Thanksgiving was not the typical holiday. Our "number 2" son and daughter-in-law, Payton and Andrea, were having a baby the following day. Andrea was going to be induced the next day, so they spent most of Thanksgiving Day together, preparing for the arrival of our first grandchild. Although we missed having them over for Thanksgiving, everyone in the family was so excited for the baby to arrive. Our youngest, Emily, lived in Boston; so she was unable to come for Thanksgiving but would make the trip home for Christmas. So it was me; my wife; and our oldest son, Dodge, celebrating together. Fewer people meant more leftovers! It was always great when any one or all of the kids could make it back home for a visit.

On the Monday prior to Thanksgiving, I had a bit of surgery; it was a tonsillectomy. I had experienced an extremely sore throat and swollen glands for much of the spring and all summer. It started to affect my speech (pushing on my tongue). The doctor sent me to a specialist who ordered a CT scan, which revealed a mass near my right tonsil. We expected the tonsillectomy to fix the problem. Needless to say, I wasn't going to be eating as usual on Thanksgiving. No turkey, no rolls, and no snacks during the football games. A little bit of mashed potatoes was the only thing on my menu. I didn't have much as I was still experiencing some discomfort from Monday's surgery.

Later that Thanksgiving night, I wasn't feeling very well. At around 8:00 p.m., I started walking down the hall to go to the bathroom. I didn't make it. On the way, my balance wasn't at its best, and I lost control of my bladder while stumbling down the hall. Yes, I peed myself. Now you might think that it is embarrassing and humiliating for a sixty-five-year-old man to pee himself. Not so! Since I have no recollection of the occurrence, I do not feel embarrassed about it one bit. (The only reason I can tell the story is because it was told to me by my wife.)

I was trembling as I felt cold; I was freezing. I finally made it to the bathroom and was standing by the sink counter. I was a mess, somewhat incoherent. My wife told me to sit on the toilet seat so she could help me with my clothes. She started fitting me with a new set of clothes, but I would not stand up. My oldest son came in and said in a commanding voice, "Get up, Dad!" There was no response. They tried to get my attention and get me to speak for a few minutes, but I did not respond. Somehow the two of them finished dressing me and got me into the car, and we headed for the local hospital's emergency room.

When we arrived at the hospital, Dodge garnered a wheelchair and wheeled me into the emergency room. They took me back into an examination area, put IVs in both arms, and gave me a COVID-19 test. My temperature was measured at 105 degrees; I was burning up! My clothes were removed, and ice packs were placed around my body. During this entire time, I was in a state of confusion. I didn't really understand what was happening. Everything seemed to take forever. A nurse would appear for a short time and say that she would "be right back," and then we wouldn't see her for such a long time. Although it seemed to take forever, I was finally taken upstairs and admitted to a hospital room.

As it turned out, I was diagnosed with aspiration pneumonia. Aspiration occurs when food, liquid, or stomach contents make their way into the airways or lungs instead of being swallowed and emptied into the stomach. If you have ever felt like you've had some food or drink that went down the wrong tube, you have experienced aspiration. Sometimes aspiration can lead to severe consequences like aspiration pneumonia. The likely outcome of aspiration pneumonia depends on one's overall health, other conditions that may be present, and how sick a person is when treatment is started. Since I had a compromised immune system because of my leukemia thirteen years earlier, aspiration pneumonia was serious business. If aspiration pneumonia goes untreated, it can be dangerous, resulting in things like lung abscesses, lung scarring, or even respiratory failure. Yes, it can even result in death.

So I spent a few days in the hospital. I met with the hospital's speech-language pathologist, who administered a swallow study. A swallow study is like an x-ray that shows a person swallowing; you can actually see the substance go down your throat on a computer monitor. After a few days, I was sent home on a pureed and thickened water diet—yum. I would say that it was a memorable Thanksgiving, but I don't remember much of what happened. My wife and son have shared what happened that night, some of which I do not recall at all, and I find it hard to believe how the events of that night actually occurred.

The surgeon who performed my tonsillectomy had removed only the left tonsil during my surgery just prior to Thanksgiving. The right tonsil was enmeshed with other tissue, so the removal of that tonsil was not possible. A tissue sample was sent off to the lab for a biopsy. The ensuing Monday, I had a follow-up appointment with the doctor who told me the biopsy showed the tissue was cancerous. *Cancer*—such a scary word! Many people freak out as soon as they hear the word *cancer*. Well, I have never been the kind of person that gets overly riled up about things. Things don't rattle me. I don't get that mad, I don't yell in anger, and I have never used profanity of any kind. Early in my career, I was a sport coach, and I prided myself on self-control and proper sideline behavior. (How can a coach expect athletes to play under control if the coach is not demonstrating a proper role model of self-control?)

I have always been a "So what's next?" kind of person. Besides, I had been through a similar experience before. Thirteen years prior to this incident, I had been diagnosed with a fairly rare form of leukemia called hairy cell leukemia. Following the leukemia scare, I often felt weak and was sick a lot. I had spent some time in the hospital with pneumonia and disseminated shingles (I had some good-sized black splotches on my hand). While in the hospital, one of the infectious disease doctors determined that I was immune-globulin deficient, which led to monthly infusions. I have been getting the monthly infusions ever since.

I had been through the process of healing before: chemotherapy, dealing with family members, facing a life-threatening illness, and much more. (At that time, one of the toughest things to deal with was seeing my eleven-year-old daughter come into my hospital room while wearing a mask; I could see the fear in her eyes, and I did not like that one bit!) An interesting sidenote: During the healing process of my leukemia scare, I had a port inserted into my chest. This allowed for easy access for medical personnel to give me medication without always having to find the best place to "stick me" with needles. One day, the nurses were unable to access my port. They sent me to a doctor who opened me up to remove the port. After making an incision, she couldn't find the catheter that was supposed to be attached to my port. It had broken off and traveled into my heart. I was lucky to be alive as the six-to-seven-inch rubber catheter sat at the bottom of the right ventricle of my heart. Long story short, a procedure the following day ended with the extraction of the catheter, even with a sustained ventricular tachycardia scare during the removal. After the procedure, the doctor in charge said I was lucky to be alive. To this day, I carry that rubber catheter as a reminder of how precious each day is.

Anyway, I had been to the cancer clinic to receive infusions for chemotherapy before. I had been poked with needles countless times, and I had experienced the complications and side effects that occur from time to time with chemotherapy. For a while, I was able to perform my infusions at home, where I stuck two needles into my belly fat and rode the recliner until the "super juice" was all in. Once I went on Medicare, I was required to receive the infusions at a doctor's office. At home, it took me about two hours and forty-five minutes for the infusions to occur. At the Office of Infectious Diseases, where I received my infusions, the juice was infused directly into a vein in my arm; and the process took almost four hours to complete the infusion. (Driving one hour and fifteen minutes each way and four hours of infusion time made my infusions a day-long experience.) My infusions have occurred every month for years. These infusions help keep me alive.

So when I heard *cancer*, my immediate reaction was "What do we need to do to fix this?" I had lots of questions like "What does the treatment entail?" "How effective is the treatment?" and "When can we start?" My initial reaction was not to concern myself with what could happen; I wanted to know what I needed to do to get well. As it turned out, my treatment didn't start for about five or six weeks, which frustrated me a bit. I was ready to get after it. Let's go! Focusing on what's next keeps one from wallowing in the possible bad things that can result from cancer. Keeping an eye on the positive is the way to go. Not only does it keep me in better spirits, but it also positively impacts those around me—friends and family. How a person responds to adversity says a lot about the person to him or herself and to others. Matthew 5:16 states,

> *In the same way, let your light shine before others,*
> *that they may see your good deeds and glorify your*
> *Father in heaven.*

Our actions matter even when we may not be happy with our circumstances. Setting an example for others, especially during trying times, can be a significant teaching tool. What a great way to teach children how to respond when the world throws them a curveball. In addition, 1 Peter 2:12 tells us,

> *Live such good lives among the pagans that, though*
> *they accuse you of doing wrong, they may see your*
> *good deeds and glorify God on the day he visits us.*

We are directed to provide a godly example for others. So when we are ailing or facing trials in life, we are instructed to demonstrate positive behavior for the good of others as well as ourselves.

The last thing people need is to hear someone complaining about how difficult their life is. Demonstrating a "woe is me" persona either turns people off or makes them assume you are a negative person. Some research has shown that the average person complains once per minute during a conversation, and research also shows that complaining is not healthy; it can cause a decline in numerous physical conditions. When we complain, neural pathways are created; and once these pathways are laid down, it becomes easier to repeat the same behavior. So complaining leads to more complaining, which leads to more complaining and so on. We must learn to practice creating new neural networks for positive, pleasant feelings instead of negative complaining. In short, be content. Famed football coach Lou Holtz said,

> *Never tell your problems to anyone...90 percent of*
> *the people don't care and the other 10 percent are*
> *glad you have them.*

He was joking…I think. But the reality is that most people do not want to hear about your problems, and even if they are willing to listen, they don't want to hear a person whine. With all kidding aside, Holtz also stated,

> *Ability is what you're capable of doing. Motivation determines what you do. Attitude determines how well you do it.*

The last part of that quote deals with attitude. Attitude determines how well we do things. Our attitude influences those around us. My attitude was going to impact my treatment and recovery. In addition, famed author of *Man's Search for Meaning* and holocaust survivor Viktor Frankl said,

> *Everything can be taken from a man but one thing: the last of the human freedoms—to choose one's attitude in any given set of circumstances, to choose one's own way.*

We always have a choice in life. We may not be able to choose our circumstances, but we do have the option to choose how we respond, which is our attitude toward life. I had a choice to make: become negative with a sour outlook that carried the "woe is me" wherever I went or have a positive attitude that demonstrated faith and hope, and yes, seek JOY. I chose JOY!

In her book *Grit: The Power of Passion and Persuasion*, Angela Duckworth defined the word *grit*.

> *Grit is that mix of passion, perseverance, and self-discipline that keeps us moving forward in spite of obstacles.*

When we find ourselves in troubled times and trials that can be life-altering (like cancer), we have the opportunity to demonstrate grit. We can overcome obstacles by adopting a grit mindset and having a passion for and the perseverance to face adversity. People notice how we act. In his first letter to the Corinthians, the apostle Paul wrote,

> *Follow my example, as I follow the example of Christ.* (1 Corinthians 11:1)

God wants us to set an example for others not when it is convenient but all the time. It is biblical to be at our best at all times.

Once the cancer diagnosis was made and November came to a close, it seemed like there was an endless stream of doctor appointments. It felt like I was in a waiting room at least every other day. It is impressive how much doctors know about our bodies and how to keep them healthy or how to heal them. Being overwhelmed with instructions and directives for the near future can lead to a negative outlook on life. So there I was, driving from one doctor appointment to another. Actually, I was being driven most of the time. (Thanks to my wife, who appears to have the love language of *acts of service*, putting others, especially me and our children, before herself; she drove me to every doctor appointment.) Heading into the Christmas season, I threw myself into positive thinking—buying presents, wrapping presents, and seeing family and friends! This cancer thing was not going to turn me into a Debbie Downer.

> *For it is by grace you have been saved, through faith—and this is not from yourselves, it is the gift of God—not by works, so that no one can boast.* (Ephesians 2:8–9)

> *I run to the Father*
> *I fall into grace*
> *I'm done with the hiding*
> *No reason to wait*
> *My heart needs a surgeon*
> *My soul needs a friend*
> *So I'll run to the Father*

Again and again
And again and again.
(Cody Carnes, "Run to the Father")

Immunodeficiency due to leukemia requires monthly infusions.

CHAPTER 2

No Cookies on Christmas Day

"It's the most wonderful time of the year"—that is what the song says. And it is. For many of us, although Christmas is on December 25, the holiday feeling lasts the entire month (or based on the displays in stores, it lasts two months or more). For me, most of the shopping for presents had been completed long before December arrived. But the wrapping of presents, the special gatherings with friends and family, the sending and receiving of Christmas cards, the food, the smell of the food, and the wonder in the faces of young kids when they see Santa or open a present that was at the top of their wish lists are what bring a glow to people's faces. Christmas is the best time of year!

Although I realize the true reason for the season is to commemorate the birth of Jesus, there are many secular elements of Christmas I enjoy: singing Christmas songs, the hustle and bustle in the stores, finding the perfect gift for someone special, Christmas stockings, and of course, Santa Claus. It seems I have always had an affinity for Santa. As a matter of fact, I have played the role of Santa many times over the years. The first time I filled the role of Santa Claus was in the school play in sixth grade. The drama was performed for the entire school (grades K-6) during the regular school day and for the parents (and families) at night. I even had to kiss Mrs. Claus (that role was played by a girl named Megan) in front of the whole school. That may have been my first kiss! By the way, I still have the same Santa hat from that play some fifty-three-plus years later, and I wear it on every Christmas morning.

In eighth grade, I was asked to play Santa for the school's girls' choir, who was going Christmas caroling at the hospital. That request was repeated in the eleventh grade. I guess someone remembered that I acted as Santa previously. Later, when I was teaching and coaching, I had my high school girls' basketball team go Christmas caroling at two local retirement centers (we used to call them old folks homes). When I was married, I served as a shopping mall Santa for two years to earn a few extra dollars. As a matter of fact, our first son's picture with Santa was of Dodge sitting on my lap at the mall. Because I had the Santa suit, I portrayed the role of Santa for a number of friends so their kids could have a fun Santa experience. When our daughter was quite young, I made the Santa visit to her preschool for a couple of years. So pretending to be Santa has been an important part of my celebration at Christmastime.

Of course, for me and many other Christians, what makes the holiday so joyful is the fact that we celebrate the birth of Jesus Christ, our Savior. Yes, the music is wonderful, but it is just a bit better when sung in a church. Gifts are great, but what better gift than that of a child who will one day sacrifice Himself for the good of all others, even those who persecuted Him? Watching special programs on TV or at the movie theater is a lot of fun, but viewing a program provided by children or the church choir for all to enjoy is the best. So yes, Christmas truly is the most wonderful time of the year…for me!

This particular December was a bit difficult for me, though. No parties or gatherings, no visits, no special foods, and no Christmas cookies! Was this really the holiday season I had come to cherish? Because of my retirement the previous spring, I had started a few new ventures. I joined the local Lions Club but was unable to participate in the holiday parade or attend the regularly scheduled meetings because of my health condition. Earlier in the year, I started volunteering at a local adult literacy program, but I had to cancel my participation. The doctor strongly recommended I impose a semi-quarantine on myself because of my compromised immune system and my new cancer diagnosis. So many typical Christmas events on my December calendar were crossed out to add various medical appointments—my primary doctor, two oncologists, a speech-language pathologist, my pulmonologist, a PET scan, an MRI, an EKG, having a feeding tube inserted into my belly, my monthly infusion of gamma globulin, blood draws, and more. Yes, it was a special month.

It was determined that I would undergo three bouts of chemotherapy sessions and thirty-five radiation treatments. There is some risk to chemotherapy and radiation treatment, and people seem to have anxiety over the risks involved with radiation. That said, although risk is a part of life, we usually want to manage our risks. I cannot remember where, but I once read that life's turmoil is not always meant to be managed. It is often meant to be embraced. Earlier in my career, I taught at the United States Military Academy at West Point. On one of my first days on post (campus), I met a lieutenant colonel who told me, "If there is risk involved, I love it!" He was always trying to get me to jump out of an airplane with him—no way! Once, Jesus was walking on the water, and when His disciples saw Him from their boat, they were afraid.

> *But Jesus immediately said to them: "Take courage!*
> *It is I. Don't be afraid."*
> *"Lord, if it's you," Peter replied, "tell me to come to*
> *you on the water."*
> *"Come," he said.*
> *Then Peter got down out of the boat, walked on the water*
> *and came toward Jesus.* (Matthew 14:27–29)

Peter was a risk-taker. We can't avoid risk in life, but we do not need to allow risk to handcuff us or make us sit in our houses in fear. Besides, sometimes, when we face risk, we are rewarded significantly. There is great satisfaction when we face and overcome risk (trials and adversity). Our confidence is bolstered, our fears are lessened, and we can experience a rise in self-esteem and efficacy.

At one of my appointments, the nurse for the radiation oncologist sat me and my wife down and tried to explain the entire chemotherapy and radiation therapy process that would be initiated in January. The nurse, Karen, was kind and seemed to be genuinely concerned about me. She kept things light until the moment when her face turned serious and, in an extremely stern voice, said, "This will be the hardest thing you have ever done." People always hear about the perils of cancer treatments—the fatigue, the episodes of nausea, the overall achiness of the body, the emotional trauma, the loss of hair, and any number of other complications because of treatment. Given all that, in the back of my mind, I was still thinking, *Really? Can it be that bad?* Well, I would find out that each individual case is different and that the severity of response to treatment could vary as well. I remember thinking, *The hardest thing I've ever done? We'll see.*

As stated earlier, I have always been a "What are we gonna do now?" kind of guy. As a former sport coach, I needed a game plan. So in my mind, I was having discussions with myself on how to approach my treatment plan. How does one prepare for such a life-altering experience? The chemotherapy and radiation treatments were scheduled to begin in January. Hey, this was early December. I wanted to get cracking on this endeavor. Why wait? Let's go! Of course, the world doesn't revolve around me, so I was going to have to wait until January. In the midst of the season of COVID-19, I was doing all I could to keep my immunodeficient body as well as possible, knowing that there was cancer growing in my throat. Masks and isolation were the ritual for me.

On December 15, a feeding tube was implanted into my abdomen. So the bulk of my food intake was through a tube that stuck out approximately seven or eight inches from my belly. At the time, I was still trying to eat a few soft foods (like Cream of Wheat); but on December 21, I participated in a video swallow study, which caused concern about the intake of any food through the mouth. This procedure was quite interesting. I was asked to ingest (and yes, swallow) four different liquids of different consistencies. One liquid was like water while the last liquid was quite thick (barium—yuck!). The speech-language pathologist was able to display my swallows on a computer monitor. It looked like an x-ray, but we could see my swallowing mechanism and the liquids going down my throat. In my case, much of the liquid was going down the wrong tube, hence my aspiration pneumonia. Once that was discovered, I was no longer to ingest any regular food through the mouth. Almost all intake was going to be through the feeding tube. Numerous boxes were delivered right to my door. These boxes contained small cartons of food substitute, a calorically dense nutrition formula. From then on, it was only liquid meals for me.

So no Christmas cookies for me (and no chips and pop during the Super Bowl later on). It wasn't too embarrassing to ingest the food substitute through the tube; I just lifted up my shirt, and my wife assisted me in getting the correct plastic syringes into the end of the tube. Then we let gravity do its thing. That means the feeding tube was held straight up, and the liquid meal was drawn through the tube because of the pull of gravity. If friends were visiting, we either waited until we could do it privately, or we gave them a show. Going out to a restaurant was out of the question. I offered to go out for a meal once in a while, knowing that I would not be eating, but my wife always declined. Once this ordeal is over and I can eat again, I owe her big-time. We will be enjoying the eating establishments in our local area on a regular basis. Not every day, but I plan on making a point to eat out more often than we used to.

Christmas was still a joyous time. All three kids plus our daughter-in-law, the new grandbaby, and my daughter's boyfriend (who eventually became her fiancé) were with us. I was trying to keep my distance from everyone, especially the baby; in my weakened condition, if I was to contract anything at all, I did not want to transfer it and infect her. So the isolation, or lack of closeness, plus the knowledge of my health issue and the added *potential of impending death because of the cancer* did affect me. I tried to be positive every single day—that's just the way I am—but it was difficult at times. That was when I could rely on my family to raise my spirits. Ultimately, I looked to God to lift me up; He would never let me down, and He was always with me! At this point, it seems appropriate to share a poem entitled "Footprints in the Sand" by Carolyn Joyce Carty:

One night a man had a dream. He dreamed
he was walking along the beach with the LORD.
Across the sky flashed scenes from his life.
For each scene he noticed two sets of
footprints in the sand: one belonging
to him, and the other to the LORD.
When the last scene of his life flashed before him,
he looked back at the footprints in the sand.
He noticed that many times along the path of
his life there was only one set of footprints.
He also noticed that it happened at the very
lowest and saddest times in his life.
This really bothered him and he
questioned the LORD about it:
"LORD, you said that once I decided to follow
you, you'd walk with me all the way.
But I have noticed that during the most
troublesome times in my life,
there is only one set of footprints.
I don't understand why when
I needed you most you would leave me."
The LORD replied:
"My son, my precious child,
I love you and I would never leave you.
During your times of trial and suffering,
when you see only one set of footprints,
it was then that I carried you."

It should be noted that there are verses in the Bible (God's Holy Word) that support this poem. Deuteronomy 1:31 states,

[A]nd in the wilderness. There you saw how <u>the</u>
<u>L</u><u>ORD</u><u> your God carried you</u>, as a father carries his

son, all the way you went until you reached this place. (Emphasis added)

Later, in Deuteronomy 31:6, it reads,

Be strong and courageous. Do not be afraid or terrified because of them, for the LORD your God goes with you; <u>he will never leave you nor forsake you</u>. (Emphasis added)

In the New Testament, Hebrews 13:5 says,

Keep your lives free from the love of money and be content with what you have, because God has said, <u>"Never will I leave you; never will I forsake you</u>." (Emphasis added)

So God would carry me whenever I faced trials and suffering, and He would always be by my side. I was never alone. This turned out to be quite important for me as I entered the radiation treatment lab or the chemotherapy room. (There are other places in the Bible that reinforce this concept; readers are encouraged to scour the Bible to find them as it could be a fun search.)

In addition to Christmas, there were other dates in the month that were a part of my health experience:

December 1	appointment with my primary caregiver
December 6	EMG test; not really related to my cancer diagnosis but was part of the screening of my neuropathy (in both legs)
December 7	appointment with oncologist (oversaw my chemotherapy)
December 10	appointment with the radiation oncologist
December 13	monthly infusion of gamma globulin because of my immunodeficiency

December 20   simulation at cancer clinic

December 21   video swallow with speech-language pathologist.

December 24   appointment for magnetic resonance imaging, or MRI (a test that produces detailed images of internal structures in the human body)

December 27   appointment (by phone) with nutritionist to discuss the process of feeding through my feeding tube.

December 29   COVID-19 test

The simulation visit was quite informative. It was a trial run to acquaint me with the treatment process. Although I had already experienced the chemotherapy lab, I had never seen or experienced the radiation area. The radiation nurse explained how things would work and the order of activities when patients showed up for treatment. My nurse also shared some things that a first-time patient may not be aware of. Practical things like where the bathrooms were, where to go when a patient first entered the lab, etc. were explained. In addition, I was given a gift bag! It had the obligatory small bottle of water, a granola bar (which I could not eat), and other odds and ends. The gift bag also included a small book titled *Jesus Calling: Enjoying Peace in His Presence* (a year-long devotional book) as well as a note of encouragement from the person who put the gift bag together. I ended up using that little devotional book each morning throughout the year; it was a great way to begin each day. (Later, during my treatment, my in-laws presented me with a nicer version of the same devotional book.) Overall, my simulation visit was informative but also meaningful to me.

So December was quite a month! Also, on the twenty-eighth of the month, I turned sixty-six years old. I never understood it when people would use the phrase "*n* years young." I have never felt old regardless of my age but didn't feel the need to tell everyone about it. I must admit that later in the spring, there were times when I did feel old. Some days felt like I had aged ten or fifteen years over the span of a week (more on this later). For my birthday, there was no cake—heaven forbid—because of my swallowing issues.

With Christmas behind us, I wanted to begin preparing for my treatment. How was I going to handle it? How could I rely on God to help me through the entire treatment process regardless of how my body responded? Over the years of attending church and Sunday school classes, many times I had come across and read James 1:2–3:

> *Consider it pure joy, my brothers and sisters, when-*
> *ever you face trials of many kinds, because you know*
> *that the testing of your faith produces perseverance.*

In my preparation for treatment, I settled in on this passage of Scripture. There were many other relevant Bible verses, but I decided to focus on this passage from the book of James. Clearly, I was facing a trial. My thoughts were trying to zero in on how my cancer and treatment (my trials) should bring me JOY. Also, if my treatment was going to test my faith, I wanted to develop the perseverance needed to help me get through the treatment. As a matter of fact, the truth that God loves me enough to want to grow me, test me, and provide me with perseverance should bring me JOY!

God loves me! He wants good things to happen in my life. That is a promise from God. He makes everything good for people who love, cherish, and honor Him. Romans 8:28 states,

> *And we know that in all things God works for the*
> *good of those who love him, who have been called*
> *according to his purpose.*

Therefore, as I was preparing to undergo treatment for my throat cancer, I knew God would use this trial to grow me. It was up to me to allow Him to work in my life. If He was using this trial to develop me, build perseverance in my life, and make me a better person, I had to find JOY in the endeavor. God keeps His promises! What I needed to do was make sure I was seeking His will and not my own. The circumstance—chemotherapy and radiation treatments—may not be to my liking, but it is part of His plan for my life. I had to believe this to maintain a positive attitude, find the JOY in each day, and beat cancer's butt!

God's handiwork—yes, He made me. One of my favorite quotes, one I used throughout my career, especially in the sport coaching field, is "Make each day your masterpiece." The quote is attributed to John Wooden, legendary basketball coach. (He won ten national championships over a span of twelve years yet never focused on winning!) That quote aligns with a verse from the New Testament.

> *For we are God's handiwork, created in Christ Jesus*
> *to do good works, which God prepared in advance*
> *for us to do.* (Ephesians 2:10)

I am God's handiwork, His masterpiece every day, every hour, and every minute! He blessed me with cancer. My job was and still is to find that blessing and revel in it. So many people have shown love and concern for me that I am amazed at how God provides JOY in our lives.

> *But the angel said to her, "Do not be afraid, Mary;*
> *you have found favor with God. You will conceive*
> *and give birth to a son, and you are to call him*
> *Jesus. He will be great and will be called the Son*
> *of the Most High. The Lord God will give him the*
> *throne of his father David, and he will reign over*
> *Jacob's descendants forever; his kingdom will never*
> *end."* (Luke 1:30–33)

> *Hark! The herald angels sing*
> *"Glory to the new-born king*
> *Peace on earth and mercy mild*
> *God and sinners reconciled"*
> *Joyful all ye nations rise*
> *Join the triumph of the skies*
> *With angelic host proclaim*
> *"Christ is born in Bethlehem"*
> *Hark! The herald angels sing*
> *"Glory to the new-born king"*
> (Charles Wesley, "Hark the Herald Angels Sing")

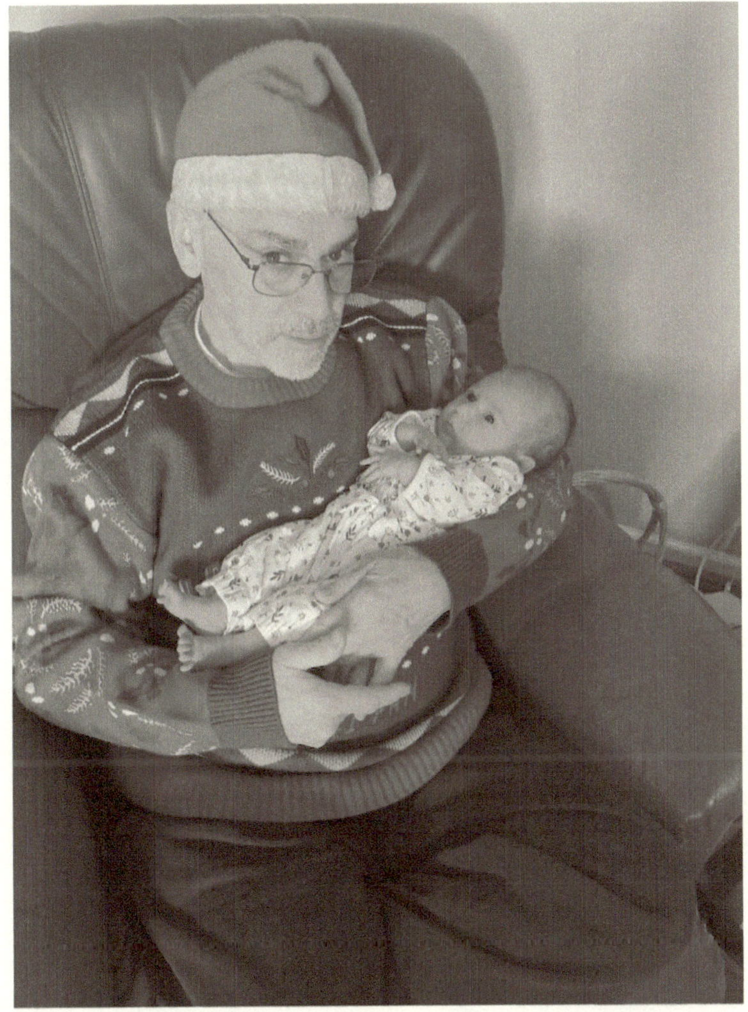

No cookies at Christmas but still finding joy with granddaughter.

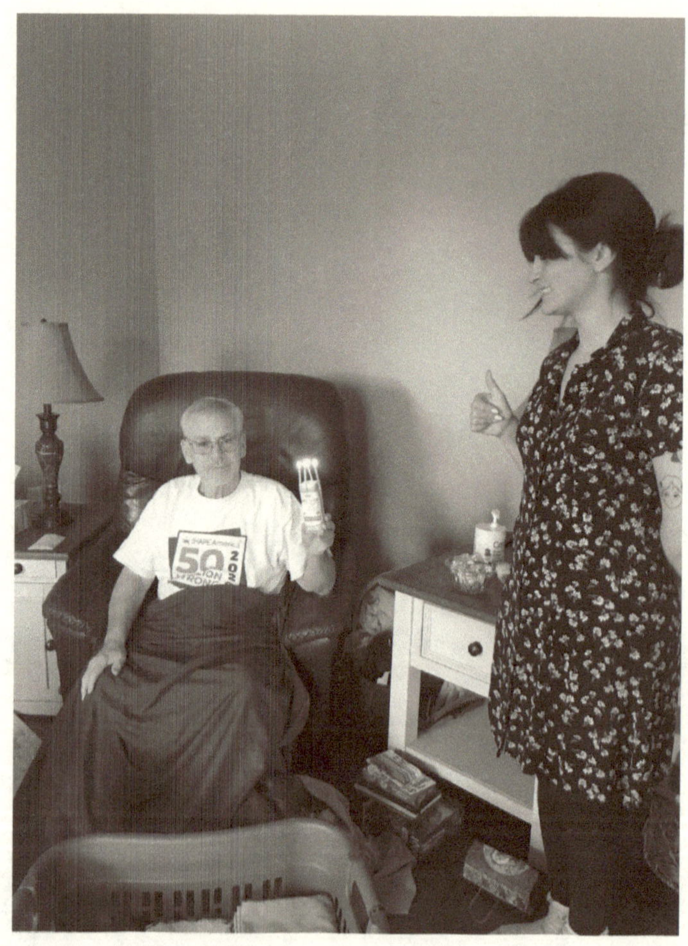

No birthday cake, so my daughter put candles on my carton of formula.

CHAPTER 3

Happy New Year

It was January 1, and everyone knows what that means: college football bowl games! Yes, there are many other bowl games during the year-end season, but January 1 is always an all-day affair. We begin with *College Game Day*, a television show that sets the table for the football games to be played that day, with added human-interest stories about players and coaches. Saturday morning is my time to enjoy football commentary at its finest. On this particular January 1, the following bowl games were scheduled:

Fiesta Bowl	Oklahoma University and the Notre Dame faced each other.
Rose Bowl	Ohio State University played the University of Utah.
Sugar Bowl	Baylor University squared off against the University of Mississippi.

What a great day of football with some exciting games (based on the scores). Of course, this year I was limited on what I could eat and drink. No chips, pop, hot dogs, or hamburgers; it was just the feeding tube.

Let's talk about the feeding tube. As stated earlier, it was embedded into my stomach on December 15. It wasn't necessarily a hassle, but it became a bit annoying at times as it was always getting in the way. I was always worried something might happen to it. "What if it comes out?"—that question created a bit of anxiety for me, so I would have to recall Philippians 4:6–7:

> *Do not be anxious about anything, but in every situation, by prayer and petition, with thanksgiving, present your requests to God. And the peace of God, which transcends all understanding, will guard your hearts and your minds in Christ Jesus.*

I shouldn't worry about the feeding tube. In the grand scheme of things, if a person was going to worry about something, there are many things that are far more serious than a feeding tube. Besides, God is in control.

> *I have told you these things, so that in me you may have peace. In this world you will have trouble. But take heart! I have overcome the world.* (John 16:33)

With God in control, I should be able to experience this trial and not be so caught up in anxiety that I am unable to focus on God. And if God tells me not to worry about things, I should listen and obey. Once I gave that concern to God, it was no longer a worrisome issue. God's promise did give me a bit of peace. Sometimes God provides a test for us. It becomes a matter of trust and faith. If I am right with God, my anxiety should vanish. As they say in New Zealand, "No worries." Yet I am human, and God loves me and protects me. Psalm 40:2 states,

> *He lifted me out of the slimy pit, out of the mud and mire; he set my feet on a rock and gave me a firm place to stand.*

No matter where I find myself, in the thick of trouble or lost, God is faithful; He is always with me. I can stand firm on His character.

One time later in the year, my feeding tube did actually come out. During the middle of the night, I rolled over in bed, and the tube got caught in the covers and was pulled out. It was no big deal. I quickly stuck it back in the hole in my stomach. The following day, we went to the hospital, and they reinserted the tube. In fact, they gave me an entirely new tube, and I learned that this was a common occurrence. Some people go into the hospital on a semiregular basis to have a new feeding tube inserted.

Every so often, a number of good-sized boxes were delivered to my doorstep. In the boxes were numerous small cartons of nutrition-packed liquid—250 ml (that's 8.45 fluid ounces) of formula. That was my breakfast, lunch, dinner, and one snack. It varied, but I consumed four or five cartons a day. I began ingesting these liquid meals, and that was all I "ate" throughout my treatment and recovery. It turned into a running joke. Every once in a while, I would look over at my wife, who was eating regular food, and say, "Mmm, this sure is good." I kind of lived vicariously through her, watching her eat while I poured my meal into my tube. The nutritionist suggested that I increase to six cartons a day, which I tried for a while, but that was just too much. This liquid diet was supposed to keep my weight up, but I lost quite a bit of weight. Prior to this entire ordeal, I weighed in at 217 pounds. (I have always been a little bit heavy, and when I had leukemia and was ingesting large quantities of steroids, I actually gained a ton of weight, tipping the scales at 256 pounds, my highest weight.) Throughout this difficult trial, I dropped a lot of weight, weighing in at 157 pounds, my lowest.

The total feeding tube assembly is a pretty simple device; a plastic syringe is inserted into a rubber tube that protrudes from the belly. Yet I often had my difficulties with it during my feedings. Sometimes, when I pulled the plug on top of the tube to open it up, it would spout out a few drops of liquid. I don't know why. It must have been built-up pressure from my gut. Also, I would sometimes forget to keep my mouth shut; I might begin talking to my wife (or the TV if a football game was on [yes, I talk to the TV]), and my talking caused fluid to come out of the tube. I had to remember to wait until the opening of the tube was closed before I started talking. Often, it was just something I forgot from time to time, which resulted in a mess. Lastly, if I wasn't paying attention, the syringe would disconnect from the tube, and I might not notice until I felt the liquid collecting in my lap. Needless to say, I was pretty sure that I was smarter than a plastic syringe and rubber tube, but I often experienced feeding-tube failures.

On January 3, my treatments began. On the first day, I had a session of chemotherapy that was followed by the first of thirty-five radiation treatments. The chemotherapy lab was full of recliners, about twenty-two to twenty-four of them. On that first day, the chemotherapy lab was about half full of patients. There were days when it was packed, but on my first day, the number of patients was fairly light. That meant more attention from the attending nurses.

It was interesting to see the different people in the lab. Some were "old pros." They had been receiving treatment for some time and were quite comfortable in their surroundings. From time to time, there were a few patients who acted like they owned the place, while others were seemingly quite tentative. Some of the new patients didn't want to do the wrong thing, go to the wrong place, or bother anyone around them. The reality was that it didn't take long for the patients in the lab to form a community, a group of people with similar issues that encouraged one another, welcomed one another, and actually became friends—"chemo buds." They had all felt the aftereffects of the chemotherapy infusions; they had all experienced the fear of the unknown; they have all dealt with their mortality; they all needed each other's help and support.

The nurses in the chemotherapy lab were "angels of mercy" that went out of their way to make patients feel comfortable when it was nearly impossible to feel comfortable. These nurses were the ones that poked you, prodded you, or brought you a warm blanket or a pillow. They even offered snacks. Nurses empathized with the patients while sticking them with a needle. The nurses that care for cancer patients, for the most part, are not people who go to their nine-to-five job to collect a paycheck. They seem to have a calling to care for others. The nurses in my particular lab made me feel like I was one of the family. Part of the healing process was not only physical, but the emotional status and feeling of well-being also contributed to the overall recovery. For me, it got to the point where I looked forward to my visit to the cancer center because of how the nurses cared for me.

So what about fear on that first day in the chemotherapy and radiation labs? For me, there was no fear. Fear serves no purpose. Being afraid does not make the situation go away. It doesn't offer any positive result or help a person cope one bit. Being afraid is a waste of energy. For me, I had experienced the chemotherapy lab before, during my leukemia treatments. But to be totally honest, there were times when a bit of apprehension arose because a patient (me) never really knew what might happen. I went into that cancer center, especially the radiation room, thinking about my commitment to James 1:2–3. Remember, I was looking for the JOY in this trial. I found some JOY in how I was treated. The nurses eased me into the process as best they could. In Isaiah 41:10, it states,

> *Do not fear, for I am with you; do not be dismayed,*
> *for I am your God. I will strengthen you and help*
> *you; I will uphold you with my righteous right hand.*

I was not alone! The chemotherapy lab had patients and nurses around me. In essence, we were on the same team, with similar health issues and a whole bunch of emotions. Later, I lay down on that radiation table with the assurance that God was with me. I prayed throughout the duration of the treatment, and it seemed to be over fairly quick. In reality, the radiation treatment didn't last that long. A little bit of prayer and a couple of songs (they had the radio going), and it was over.

As I get older and health issues try to intrude on my way of life, the more I realize that God is in charge. He is always right there with me. Every day, I am grateful for all the blessings in my life, not only positive things but negative things too. It is easy to be thankful for His grace, mercy, love, and forgiveness; but what about the hard things that occur in life? Sometimes negative things happen to us to grow us and develop us as people. When trials come our way, we should be pleased that God loves us enough to want to grow us and draw us closer to Him. Maybe the sole purpose of the trial is to make us rely totally on God, trust Him more, demonstrate faith in Him more. We may not like the circumstance (nobody likes cancer), but we can see the positive results from the negative situation. That is how I was thinking when I entered the cancer clinic that first visit on January 3.

> *Sometimes, you must hurt in order to grow, fall in order to know, and lose in order to gain. Our greatest life lessons are learned through the hills and valleys of our own unique journey.* (Author unknown; retrieved from Facebook on August 17, 2022)

It may be interesting to share some information about the treatment process. The chemotherapy is pretty straightforward. You go in and sit in a chair, and the nurse puts a needle in your arm and fills you up with medication, what I always called super juice. Some people have a port inserted in their bodies, usually in a place with fewer nerve receptors, to make the insertion of needles easier. Typically, having a port put in may depend on the number of treatments prescribed. In my case, this time around, I did not have a port as I only had to undergo three chemotherapy treatments. Back when I had leukemia, I had a port put in to handle the infusions of medicine. At that time, my port actually led me to have a traumatic experience. The port broke; the rubber tube attached to the port, which was inserted into a vein in my chest, broke away from the port and travelled right into my heart. It squeezed its way through the upper chamber and lodged itself into the lower ventricle. With each heartbeat, my body was trying to move the rubber catheter out of my heart. Once this was discovered, it had to be removed the following day. Interestingly, the doctor inserted a device into a vein in my upper leg (near the groin), went up to the heart, secured the rubber tube, and pulled it out. He had a difficult time, and they were prepping my neck for an attempt from a different angle when he was finally successful in grasping the catheter.

The radiation treatment was foreign to me. During the simulation visit, I was fitted for a mask. The mask covered me from the top of my head to about eight to ten inches down onto my chest and shoulders. A mask was molded to my face by placing the wetted surface over me and then sucking all of the water out of it. It created a mold that perfectly fit my face and only my face. So when I entered the radiation treatment room and lay on the table, the mask was placed over me and locked into place. There were nine places where the mask was snapped into place to hold me still. The mask holds the patient in place for the radiation to be administered in specific places; it is an exact science. At first, it was quite uncomfortable; it actually hurt a bit. But it was something I got used to…kind of. With the mask on, the radiation machine moved about my head and neck to "zap" me where I needed it. The radiation process didn't take long; at most, it took fifteen minutes once I was snapped in.

Therapy day number 2 included radiation treatment only. It was an eye-opener. Or maybe I should say it was an eye closer. My eyes were closed for two reasons: 1) the mask was quite tight and pushed my eyes nearly closed, and (2) I spent much of the time praying during my treatment. The mask that was made for me felt tighter today than the first day of treatment. In addition to pushing my eyes nearly closed, the mask choked me a little bit. I thought that maybe the mask might loosen up a little with wear during the treatment, but I soon realized that didn't make any sense. The whole point of the mask was to hold me steady…that meant stiff! I thought I could tough it out. I didn't want the technicians to think I was a wimp. Anyway, toward what I thought was the end of the treatment, it became difficult to breathe. Eventually, I could barely breathe through my mouth at all. Sometimes I have difficulty breathing out through my nose, so I was beginning to feel a bit nervous.

Although I thought the end of the "zapping" was near, I tried to call out to the technicians, "I can't breathe." I said it a couple of times, but since my voice was muffled and the technicians were in a separate room, I couldn't be heard. Finally, the treatment was over.

I told one of the technicians about the tightness of my mask. "Oh, no problem," she said. "We can trim a little off around the mouth." I was also reminded of my ability to communicate with my hands, if necessary, during a treatment. I found out that all I had to do was wave my hand, and they would respond immediately. Anyway, treatment number 2 was in the books. Thirty-three more to go!

The ride home was a little more eventful that the previous day. I got the hiccups! Now I had heard about all the side effects of chemotherapy and radiation treatments. Some of the side effects include nausea, fatigue, mouth sores, loss of appetite, weight loss, and hair loss—most people have heard of these. In addition, another couple of side effects are neuropathy and something called chemo brain. Briefly, neuropathy is damage or dysfunction to one or more nerves that typically may result in numbness, tingling, muscle weakness, and pain in the affected area. Neuropathy often begins in the hands or feet, but other parts of the body may be affected. I had already been afflicted with neuropathy in both of my lower legs and needed a walker or cane to move about safely. (Recently, I have begun using trail hiking sticks to get from one place to another.) Chemo brain may result in disorganized behavior or thinking, confusion, or memory loss or may cause trouble with concentration, paying attention, and decision-making. It can occur before, during, or after cancer treatment.

My hiccups began after we had driven about a mile from the cancer center. It was hiccups; no big deal, right? Well, the hiccups continued…and continued…and continued. Each day we had to drive about fifty miles (one way) to the cancer center. As we were pulling into our hometown of Warrensburg, Missouri, the hiccups finally stopped. I had the hiccups for about forty-eight miles! After a little research, we found out that hiccups are an actual side effect of cancer treatment. As a matter of fact, there is something called intractable hiccups, when the hiccups last longer than one month in duration. I guess I got lucky!

Treatment number 3 went a little better than the day before even though the hiccups showed up again. The radiation technicians had trimmed a little off my mask, making it much easier to breathe during the radiation treatment process. I quickly learned that while going through treatment, it was helpful to find any kind of encouragement to help me get through the procedure, whatever it may be. Some people read books, while some listen to music. Some pray and read their Bibles, and of course, there are many other avenues to look for encouragement. While lying on the table this particular day, I thought of a song that was playing on the car radio during our drive to the cancer center. Here are the words to the chorus of "You Say," sung by Lauren Daigle:

> *You say I am loved when I can't feel a thing;*
> *You say I am strong when I think I am weak.*
> *And you say I am held when I am falling short;*
> *When I don't belong, oh You say I am Yours.*
> *And I believe.*

Knowing that God loves me and holds on to me helped a lot during my treatments more than I can describe. Even when I couldn't feel anything (maybe I couldn't feel His presence), knowing that He was with me gave me strength—yes, even when I was weak. Sometimes it is during times of weakness when His strength is most meaningful. During times when I didn't feel like I belonged, when I may have felt alienated for some reason, He was with me. I was not alone.

This concept is supported by many Scripture verses. For example, 2 Corinthians 12:9–10:

> *But he said to me, "My grace is sufficient for you, for*
> *my power is made perfect in weakness." Therefore I*
> *will boast all the more gladly about my weaknesses,*
> *so that Christ's power may rest on me. That is why,*
> *for Christ's sake, I delight in weaknesses, in insults,*
> *in hardships, in persecutions, in difficulties. For*
> *when I am weak, then I am strong.*

I had to remember to trust God and remember exactly who He is. God is the Creator of the universe. He is all-powerful and all-knowing. Yet this wonderful Lord of all is still interested in little old me. He cares about me, He listens to me, and He watches over me. He is my constant companion even when I don't feel His presence. Most importantly, during my cancer treatments, He gave me strength. Yes, God tests people, but He never gives us a trial or test that is too difficult for us to overcome. That means that when I face adversity, I <u>know</u> I can endure the trial and grow from it. He doesn't give me more than I can handle. First Corinthians 10:13 says,

> *No temptation has overtaken you except what is common to mankind. And God is faithful; he will not let you be tempted beyond what you can bear. But when you are tempted, he will also provide a way out so that you can endure it.*

There is a whole lot of blessings packed into that one verse, and there is JOY in seeing adversity as an opportunity to draw nearer to God.

Treatment number 4 was tolerable, although my mask did feel tight again. Nothing to complain about, but the tightness did make the treatment session a bit difficult. It may be interesting to note that I was seeing the same few ladies (other patients) at the cancer center just prior to my treatments. When patients arrive at the clinic for chemotherapy, they usually wait in the waiting room to be called for their treatment. However, those receiving radiation go directly into its own waiting area. The chemotherapy room can handle over twenty people at once; there are that many recliners. But there is only one radiation table, so fewer people are scheduled. Sometimes there is a bit of a backup of patients waiting their turn. The waiting area for radiation is not very large. It also seemed as if some patients were scheduled at the same time each day, so once patients arrived, it was only natural to talk to one another. We were all in this together! Interestingly enough, in my case, the other patients were always ladies whose ages spanned quite a few years—from thirty-something to one lady who was in her nineties.

The drive to and from the clinic had turned out to be a bit of a blessing. Although it would have been nice to have the clinic closer to home, it was just far enough to make it a bit special. My wife did all the driving. We didn't think it would be safe for me to drive. In addition to responding to the treatment, I was also experiencing some heavy-duty coughing from time to time. The cough was so severe that I could not drive safely if a coughing spree occurred. Once the hiccups ended, I often fell asleep, with the radio tuned in to our favorite Christian radio station. The music was soothing, and it kept my mindset in the right place—being worshipful toward God.

On the return drive home from the cancer center that day, the hiccups made their appearance again, and I ended up with a bit of a bellyache. Once we arrived home, there were a couple of greeting cards in the mailbox, offering prayers and support. What an uplifting moment when I wasn't feeling too well. People cared enough to take the time to secure a greeting card and mail it to me. That gave me JOY! Over time, I was amazed at the number of cards, texts, and phone calls I received, all offering support. And sometimes there were gift cards (and occasionally cash) included! Driving fifty miles each way every day for thirty-five days takes a lot of gas. With the gas prices rising, it was nice of people to provide the financial support that helped me and my family so much.

I had started writing in a journal about my experiences. It was intended to give me an opportunity to express my feelings, thoughts, hopes, and fears. I have never been much of a journal person, but writing things down helped me clear my head, express my thoughts, and relax. Even though nobody would ever read it, the process of thinking about and writing my thoughts gave me a chance to clarify some things in my mind. I usually ended each journal entry with a written prayer. The prayers weren't too long, but they kept my focus in the right place—on God. I did notice that my handwriting was getting a bit jittery. Messy writing bothers me. In the past, I always had nice penmanship (when I wanted to). For me, it was a matter of caring about the product. Unless you are writing a prescription, handwriting should be clear and easy to read. In this case, my shakiness was probably because of the treatment, coupled with some of the medications that I was taking. I didn't worry about it; nobody was going to see it. My purpose in journaling was to collect my thoughts and work through the mental and emotional elements of the treatment process.

The fifth and final treatment of the week went pretty well. The day was cold (January 7 in Missouri), but at least there was no snow on the ground. Yes, it was cold; and I felt tired, was a bit jittery, and had a bit of a bellyache. But it could have been a lot worse. NO COMPLAINTS! I woke up that day! It was a good day for a good day. And no hiccups!

The whole radiation process seemed easier that day. The mask fit well; my face didn't feel as if it was smashed into it. And the time seemed to go fast. Soon after I took my position on the radiation treatment table, I felt like I was getting back up and walking out the door. I wondered if I fell asleep. It went so well that I remember thinking, *Hey, I've got this. No problem.* Then I realized that this was the end of week one, with six weeks to go. That meant thirty more radiation treatments. It was going to be a long haul.

I remember feeling grateful for those taking care of me—the nurses, the technicians, and my wife. Too often, people take simple things for granted, like walking into the kitchen to get a drink of water. Not me. Not anymore. It is the people who take care of us that bring us what we need, whether it be a glass of water, our shoes, our medicine, etc. that make getting through this process manageable. God gives us so much. He provides for our needs and then some. We need to count our blessings and recognize where they come from.

> *And my God will meet all your needs according to the riches of his glory in Christ Jesus.* (Philippians 4:19)

> *If you then, who are evil, know how to give good gifts to your children, how much more will your Father who is in heaven give good things to those who ask him!* (Matthew 7:11)

Consider the ravens: They do not sow or reap, they have no storeroom or barn; yet God feeds them. And how much more valuable you are than birds! (Luke 12:24)

When upon life's billows you are tempest-tossed,
When you are discouraged, thinking all is lost,
Count your many blessings, name them one by one,
And it will surprise you what the Lord hath done.

Count your blessings, name them one by one,
Count your blessings, see what God has done!
(Johnson Oatman Jr., "Count Your Blessings")

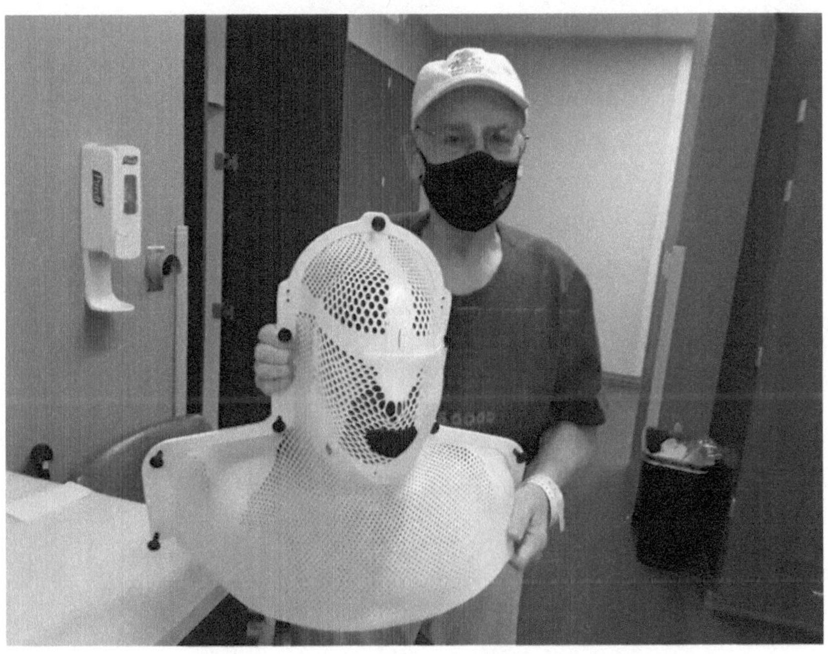

My radiation mask.

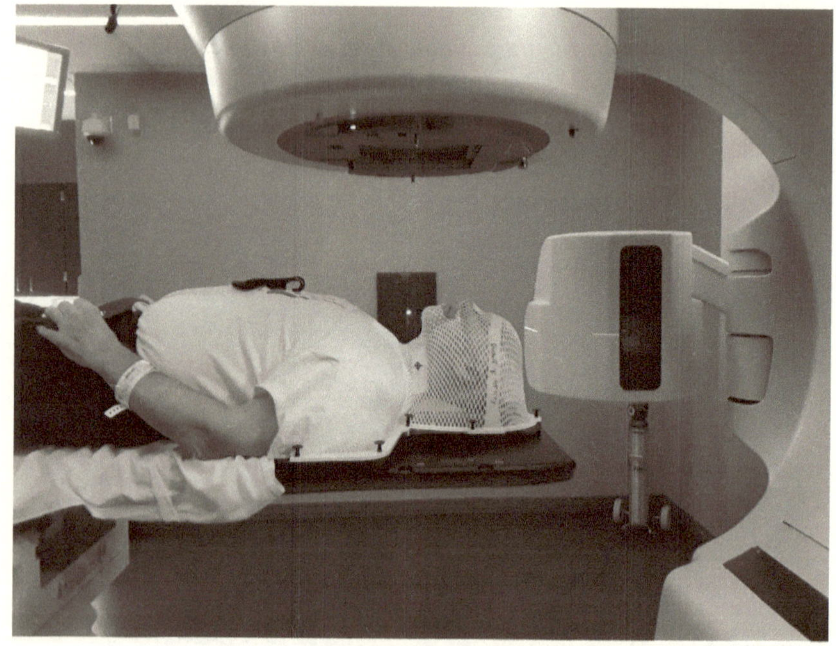

Lying on the radiation table, locked in.

Chapter 4

Be Strong and Courageous

For many years, I was a sport coach. I coached at the middle school, high school, and collegiate levels. I also coached multiple sports—football, basketball, track and field, volleyball, and golf (volleyball and golf were only for one season). Fun note: I was asked to fill in for the normal golf coach, who was completing his master's degree. I was NOT a golf coach. I was not even a golfer. I was a "hacker." But the athletic director knew I would monitor the kids and get them where they needed to be on time. Anyway, that year, the team won its first league championship in the school's history. Go figure. When coaching young people, I always tried to include the "outside of sport" element—in other words, what I (we coaches) taught the athletes applied to their lives away from the playing arena—teaching things like developing positive character, responsibility, sacrifice, "team before me" concepts, dedication, and so much more. Coaches often use inspirational quotes from others to spur athletes to go beyond their normal efforts. One of my favorite quotes comes from legendary football coach Bill Walsh:

The four most powerful words are: I believe in you.

One of the unique things about Bill Walsh was that he was a head football coach at the high school, college, and professional levels. I always liked him because although he worked tirelessly to win football games, coaching was more than just about the game. He taught life skills to athletes, even at the professional level. For a moment, imagine if teachers and coaches would say, "I believe in you" to their students and athletes just prior to their contests. Imagine parents using this phrase with their children as they were entering middle school or high school. Imagine if people said, "I believe in you" to themselves. Everyone would feel better about themselves, be more confident, perform better, and probably be more successful. Those are four powerful words! At the end of this chapter, Coach Walsh's "Standard of Performance" is shared. It is being included for a couple of reasons: (1) it is excellent, and (2) it can apply to almost any profession or life situation. The reader is encouraged NOT to skip it, whether they are a fan of sport coaches or not.

So the former coach in me—who spent many years trying to teach, inspire, encourage, and push players—entered the second week of treatment, trying to coach myself up! How might I coach myself? Inspire myself? Push and encourage myself? This was not going to be easy. I looked at quotes from the coaching world, especially those from coaches I admired. I found stories of people who overcame adversity. I looked at other times in my life when I made it through difficult stretches. Recall that during one of my early appointments, a radiation nurse told me, "This is going to be the hardest thing you have ever done." I had to find that inner strength and courage that helps people overcome adversity. Then I reminded myself that God was with me. In Joshua 1:6–7, 9, God said,

> *Be strong and courageous, because you will lead these people to inherit the land I swore to their ancestors to give them. Be strong and very courageous. Be careful to obey all the law my servant Moses gave you; do not turn from it to the right or to the left, that you may be successful wherever you go. Have I not commanded you? Be strong and courageous. Do*

not be afraid; do not be discouraged, for the LORD
your God will be with you wherever you go.

Later, in the New Testament, Jesus said,

Peace I leave with you; my peace I give you. I do not
give to you as the world gives. Do not let your hearts
be troubled and do not be afraid. (John 14:27)

Notice that within these verses, God says to be strong and courageous three times. When God speaks, we need to listen. When He repeats Himself, we need to pay special attention. If He comes around a third time, book it! This is a <u>command</u> that we must listen to and obey. I needed to be strong and courageous not for myself but because God was instructing me (us) to be strong and courageous. And remembering that He is with me (us) all along the way makes it a whole lot easier to be strong and courageous, look adversity in the face, and see opportunity! We can have trust and hope in God because He is faithful. He keeps His promises. Be encouraged to read the following Bible verses as if they are a promise from God to us (me and you) that He is with us (me and you) at all times.

God is faithful, who has called you into fellowship with
his Son, Jesus Christ our Lord. (1 Corinthians 1:9)

But the Lord is faithful, and he will strengthen you and
protect you from the evil one. (2 Thessalonians 3:3)

So then, those who suffer according to God's will
should commit themselves to their faithful Creator
and continue to do good. (1 Peter 4:19)

There is more, but I don't need to be hit over the head. I trust God! He loves me and watches over me. That fact makes me strong and courageous.

Most people know the story of David and Goliath. Regardless of whether coaches are men or women of faith, they often refer to David and Goliath when their teams are facing stronger opponents. I encourage the reader to review 1 Samuel 17 for the inspirational story. But is it just a story? Or is it true? I believe the story of David and Goliath to be a true event. Now let's think about the specifics of the story. Goliath was the champion of the Philistines, standing at nine feet and nine inches tall and weighing around six hundred pounds. His body armor weighed approximately 140 pounds (probably more than David weighed). He stood in front of the Israelite army and challenged anyone of them to fight, one against one. Each one of the Israelites was afraid. David was a shepherd boy, probably a young teenager. David volunteered to fight the Philistine.

So Goliath was in full armor, with his sword and spear, while David showed up wearing no armor and carried only five stones and a slingshot. When Goliath saw David, he laughed and mocked the young shepherd boy. But David showed no fear. He shouted,

> *You come against me with sword and spear and javelin, but I come against you in the name of the* LORD *Almighty, the God of the armies of Israel, whom you have defied.* (1 Samuel 17:45)

He added,

> *All those gathered here will know that it is not by sword or spear that the* LORD *saves; for the battle is the* LORD'S, *and he will give all of you into our hands.* (1 Samuel 17:47)

As Goliath approached, David pulled out one of his stones, placed it in his sling, gave it a few swings, and let the rock fly. The projectile hit Goliath in the forehead, stopping him in his tracks. It only took one shot—no practice, no warm-up, no worries.

The point is David showed no fear because his Lord God Almighty was with him. He was protected. Well, my Goliath was throat cancer. I did not have to fight on my own. God was with me. I did not have to bow down to cancer. Romans 8:35 states,

> *Who shall separate us from the love of Christ? Shall trouble or hardship or persecution or famine or nakedness or danger or sword?*

I did not need to fear trouble, hardship, persecution, famine, nakedness, sword…or cancer. God would prevail regardless of the outcome. He was in control. I had to remind myself of this fact over and over again.

My second week of treatment began like a bumpy road; it was hard. It seemed like I was going to choke during my treatment on Monday. As a result of my radiation blast for the day, I felt discomfort, my throat hurt, I was slurring my speech a bit, and I didn't sleep well. My wife reminded me of what the doctors and nurses told me: these reactions were to be expected. So if I could expect the troublesome effects, I could better deal with them. This was my chance to turn adversity into opportunity. Rely on God. Lean on Him. Be strong and courageous. Jesus said,

> *Come to me, all you who are weary and burdened, and I will give you rest.* (Matthew 11:28)

Imagine a person working out in a fitness facility, sweating, hurting, and pushing him- or herself. Now imagine a personal trainer standing over and encouraging that person every step of the way: "Come on, you can do it. Don't give up. I am with you." Well, Jesus served as my personal trainer. I imagined Him standing over me, supporting and encouraging me: "Come on, Dennis, you can do it. Don't give up. I am with you. I believe in you!"

I must insert a note here about two professional colleagues who called me on the telephone on the previous Sunday night. Not only did these two ladies provide encouraging words, which gave me such a positive lift, but they also prayed for me over the phone. We all need friends like that. These ladies deserved a hug! It is amazing how little effort it takes to lift up those in need. A simple phone call or dropping a card in the mail can make an ailing person's day. Even if you cannot make a call, mail a greeting card, or send an email, offering a simple prayer of healing can work wonders (and the person offering the prayer receives benefits too).

I was a little concerned about my weight; I was only 176 pounds on Tuesday. (The last time I weighed 176 was fifty years ago; I was a sophomore in high school.) I had lost the ability to taste. I was also beginning to have difficulty swallowing, so the choices of food was even more limited than before. My wife made me a smoothie that morning, and I tasted nothing. Also, my favorite breakfast, Cream of Wheat, was no longer enjoyable; it felt like I was eating sand. Swallowing was becoming more difficult and dangerous; the threat of aspiration pneumonia was ever present. I vowed to myself to remember this when I became healthy and able to eat again: TAKE NOTHING FOR GRANTED; APPRECIATE ALL BLESSINGS! It was getting to the point where I couldn't eat anything; all intakes would be through the feeding tube.

The second day of treatment for the week provided more discomfort, especially in the right side of my jaw. The swelling in my face and jaw was concerning to me. My jaw seemed to want to hang down a bit. Most people may not have noticed since we were all wearing our masks because of COVID-19, but the swelling was quite pronounced. We met with the radiology oncologist after my treatment that Tuesday. He said that everything was going well. I believed him because I had nothing to compare things to. I told him that the sores in my mouth were bothersome. He said that was to be expected and gave me a prescription for some "magic mouthwash" to help ease the sting in my mouth. I used it each morning. It worked for a little while, but the pain always returned.

I felt thirsty…a lot! Since the radiation put my salivary glands to rest, a dry mouth was a constant. It would have been nice to grab a glass of water or down some soda pop, but no such luck. So I needed to remember to nourish myself even if it was through the feeding tube. The feeding tube was fairly simple, especially when I was only filling up with water. I could do it by myself, but I loved it when my wife helped me. She is not only my wife, best friend, and forever partner, but she is also my no. 1 caregiver. Caring for me is right in her wheelhouse; her love language seems to be acts of service. I thank God for her every single day. She is a gift from God.

I also thank Keri. I do so every day. "Thanks for marrying me" has become a daily utterance. When I send her a text or email, I almost always include a TFMM. Think about that for a moment. If people would say, "Thanks for marrying me" (or some equivalent phrase) to their partners every single day—AND TRULY MEAN IT—imagine the peace that would be in those homes. There is no need for arguments, raised voices, or selfish behavior. It may seem awfully simple, but it works!

Although the next treatment day was still difficult, the routine was becoming a tad bit easier to handle. On Wednesday, I went into the radiation lab with the proper mindset. I was thinking of Philippians 4:13:

I can do all things through Him who strengthens me.

Also, I was remembering my focus for the entire treatment experience from James 1:2, trying to find the JOY in my trial. The treatment was hard. It should be hard. But it wasn't me that was getting me through the treatment. It was Jesus. My day was consumed with cancer—medications, feedings, lotioning up my dry skin, pain killers, etc. It continued all day long, but it was doable. I could not allow my Goliath to overtake me. Cancer could not defeat me. Christ was carrying me through it.

That said, I wanted the treatments to be over. But with twenty-seven treatments to go, I knew I needed to be patient. It is interesting to note that patience is something we all need and want. There is nobody who will ever say, "I want less patience." Some people pray for patience, yet when opportunities for them to practice patience arise, they get flustered instead of practicing the patience they asked for. When people want patience, they want it right now! They even get angry with God because He "takes too long" when patience does not arrive on their timeline. Second Peter 3:9 tells us:

> *The Lord is not slow in keeping his promise, as some understand slowness. Instead he is patient with you, not wanting anyone to perish, but everyone to come to repentance.*

So God's timing is perfect. When we complain or whine about Him taking too long, we forget that just maybe He was the one that arranged the issues that required our patience. As problems arise, instead of practicing patience, we get angry; and it is our impatience that falls short of the mark. James 1:19–20 tells us,

> *My dear brothers and sisters, take note of this: Everyone should be quick to listen, slow to speak and slow to become angry, because human anger does not produce the righteousness that God desires.*

Why do we get angry with God? It seems a bit arrogant to be mad at the Creator of the universe, especially since He only wants us to grow nearer to Him. We get what we ask for (e.g., opportunities to practice patience), and then we blow it.

I was not going to be cured of cancer in one day or one week. It takes time. Maybe the length of time required to be healed might bring a greater reward. In today's world, people live in the NOW. When someone needs something, they want instant results. It is a microwave world—instant coffee, instant food, instant results, instant everything! The attention spans of people are getting shorter and shorter; there is a lack of "stick-with-it-ness" all around us. It doesn't work that way with cancer. Treatment takes time, and I felt that the treatments were doing something. I could feel it in my neck during my radiation treatments. My body was responding. The effects of the radiation were not always pleasant, but it should have been a sign that things were happening. Since I could feel something was going on in my throat, I knew I could endure the trial of my treatments.

As the second week of treatment ended, the mouth sores were constantly causing issues. Discomfort was expected, but my lips and gums were in endless pain. However, I seemed to fall into the treatment routine, which made everything appear to go a little smoother. There is a bit of comfort in finding a routine if we can keep the routine from turning into boredom. Meeting and waiting with the other patients prior to treatment created a bond among us. It was nice seeing other patients. One in particular, let's call her Kate, was ninety-three years old and a bit of a jokester. After about the third day, she said to me, "We've got to stop meeting like this." During the second week, she referred to me as her "boyfriend." There was some kind of comfort in knowing that others were going through the same thing I was experiencing. But when you go into the lab and lie down on the radiation table, you are all on your own. For me, prayer was covering my time on the slab. I truly believed that Jesus was with me when the radiation mask went on. I trusted in His loyalty. He promised to be with me, and He was.

I was especially enjoying the rides home from the cancer clinic. Usually, I would suggest that my wife stop and get a drink or sandwich (or French fries). She would say, "No thanks," and we would drive on. In a matter of minutes, we were headed down the highway. Once we hit the highway, I would turn on the radio to our favorite Christian station, and about thirty-five or forty minutes later, I would wake up. Sleep came easy on the drive home. I wish it was that way at nighttime. It didn't take long before I was sleeping my way home. It was the radiation; it zapped me—literally. The zapping of the radiation zapped my strength, mind, and entire body.

> *Your kingdom is an everlasting kingdom, and your dominion endures through all generations. The* Lord *is trustworthy in all he promises and faithful in all he does.* (Psalm 145:13)

Whatever I face
Whatever the fear
Whatever the cost
You always draw near;
Whatever the pain
Whatever may come
Whatever may fall
Your love overcomes.
(Adrienne and Jeremy Camp, "Whatever May
    Come")

Bill Walsh's Standard of Performance

Exhibit a ferocious and intelligently applied work ethic directed at continual improvement; demonstrate respect for each person in the organization and the work he or she does; be deeply committed to learning and teaching, which means increasing your own expertise; be fair; demonstrate character; honor the direct connection between details and improvement, and relentlessly seek the latter; show self-control, especially where it counts most—under pressure; demonstrate and prize loyalty; use positive language and have a positive attitude; take pride in my effort as an entity separate from the result of that effort; be willing to go the extra distance for the organization; deal appropriately with victory and defeat, adulation and humiliation (don't get crazy with victory nor dysfunctional with loss); promote internal communication that is both open and substantive (especially under stress); seek poise in myself and those I lead; put the team's welfare and priorities ahead of my own; maintain an ongoing level of concentration and focus that is abnormally high; and make sacrifice and commitment the organization's trademark. (The Score Takes Care of Itself: My Philosophy of Leadership, 2009)

My answer to prayer: Keri is a gift from God.

CHAPTER 5

The Happiest Place on Earth

Contrary to what many people believe, there can be no argument as to what the happiest place on earth is. Some people may contend that the happiest place is their preferred golf course or their favorite comfortable chair while reading a good book. Others might argue that the happiest place on earth is Grandma's lap or their favorite campsite in the middle of a forest. There are many potential happy places, but we must agree that the happiest place on earth is Disneyland (not Disney World; Disneyland is the original). It has to be so. They advertise it as such, so it must be true. I have read the signs while entering the Magic Kingdom.

As a youngster, I grew up not too far from Disneyland. I was told that my favorite ride was the Matterhorn. It was fast and made quick turns. I could go on the ride again and again, and it would not be enough. Least favorite ride? For me, I can do without It's a Small World. Eventually, the song gets to me, and I want to go back to the Matterhorn and throw myself off the mountain. Anyway, here is a Disneyland story. On the Jungle Cruise ride, people sit in a boat that meanders down the river, encountering many "wild" animals. There are elephants, tigers, crocodiles, and many more. On this particular day, I was young enough to believe that the hippos and other animals seen during the Jungle Cruise ride were real. For me, the scariest were the hippos that would rise up out of the water with their mouths wide open. Once, the driver of our tour boat yelled, "Look out!" pulled a pistol, and shot at one of the hippos. The hippo dropped back into the water. I was sitting in the very back corner of the boat when the giant head came up out of the water. It was SO BIG and SO CLOSE and looked SO REAL that I thought I was a goner. It seemed so real. But of course, we made it back to land safely.

Later, our family was gathered near the Dumbo ride. Next to the Dumbo ride, there was an eating establishment called Captain Hook's, as I recall. The restaurant was surrounded by a lake of water. As we enjoyed a few snacks, I dropped my popcorn into the water. While I reached for the popcorn, my sandal fell off my foot and landed in the lagoon. My sandal began to float away, so I reached really far to retrieve it. Then I tumbled into the lake. When I hit the water, the first thing that entered my mind was the Jungle Cruise ride. I knew one of those mean hippos was going to get me! I was thrashing about, knowing that I was facing certain death. My dad reluctantly stepped into the water and pulled me out to safety. He was not pleased. He had my mom take me to the ladies' restroom to try and dry me off. Then I was put in the car and spent the rest of the day there…alone.

Truth be told, the lake water was clear, like bathwater, and only about a foot to a foot and a half deep. More truth: Having to spend the rest of the day in the car by myself is disputed by some family members. (I was told that I misremember the detail about being left alone in the car, but my version of the story makes my point.) Details…they don't really matter in this case. The point is that I felt upset and alone at Disneyland that day. Having to be dragged into the ladies' restroom to be toweled off was so embarrassing, and being left alone in the car (or just the thought of being left alone) was a horrible thing. This was no longer the happiest place on earth. I felt all alone.

Is it possible for the radiation table to be the happiest place on earth? Of course not! Is it possible that the cancer center is the Magic Kingdom? If my claim is true, that Jesus was with me on that table, shouldn't I be happy? Shouldn't I feel elated? Shouldn't I experience JOY? Some might think this is ridiculous, but there is a principle involved. I was not alone on that table (just like I was not alone in that car). Jesus was with me; He was holding my hand. I may not have seen Him or felt Him, but He was there. He was carrying me through the trial. All I had to do was call on Him and hold on. The words to the chorus of a song, "Hold On to Me," seem appropriate here:

> *Hold on to me when it's too dark to see You*
> *When I am sure I have reached the end*
> *Hold on to me when I forget I need You*
> *When I let go, hold me again.*

These words, sung by Lauren Daigle, may be suitable for a prayer while going through a cancer treatment or experiencing any kind of trial. When we are at our worst or when we face any kind of adversity, He is with us. We need to remember that. In Matthew 28:19–20, Jesus was speaking,

> *Therefore go and make disciples of all nations, bap-*
> *tizing them in the name of the Father and of the*
> *Son and of the Holy Spirit, and teaching them to*
> *obey everything I have commanded you. And surely*
> *I am with you always, to the very end of the age.*

Notice that in the last line, He makes the claim that He is with us until the end of time. If He is with us until the "very end of the age," then He was with me when I was lying on the radiation table (or wherever I am during any trial). Jesus is ALWAYS with us. That should give us JOY! Knowing that the Creator and Lord of everything chooses to hold on to us, especially during those difficult times, should give us assurance. We can make it. We can survive. We can be at the happiest place on earth…wherever we are! Remember the poem "Footprints in the Sand," provided in chapter 2? Yes, I was being carried by my Lord and Savior, Jesus Christ, just as He carries all of us through trials every single day.

The third week of treatment was abbreviated because of a holiday on Monday: Martin Luther King Day. My weight was not going up! Maybe that was what the radiation oncologist meant when he said, "Eating is a full-time job." My feeding tube had become my road to sustainability. With swallowing being such a struggle, even a tiny sip of water was difficult, so I needed to maintain my feeding schedule. I had upped my feedings to five times per day, but maybe I needed six. The entire feeding process does create a significant interruption throughout the day, but what else did I have to do, right? (By the way, my feeding tube leaked the other day—gross.)

The mouth sores were still causing issues for me. Some discomfort was expected, but my lips and gums were in constant pain. It really was annoying. Somewhere I heard or read that insignificant pain should not get in the way of recovery. The pain in my mouth was not directly associated with the cancer; it was probably a response to the radiation. A mouth full of sores was only a distraction. Maybe that was why the sore lips and gums were there—to distract me from the actual treatment. Should I have been pleased about the pain in my mouth? If I consider the sores and pain as resulting from the killing of my cancer, there should have been pleasure in those sores! They might even be another source of JOY.

Treatment number 11 went well. It might have been my best day on the radiation table. I had settled into the routine, the zapping went by without any issues, and the time on the table seemed to fly by. I was really trying to maintain a focus on God during my treatments. He made my burdens light. He was with me when the mask went on, He was with me when the radiation was entering my body, and He was with me when the oxycodone didn't make all the pain go away. In the middle of the night, when I couldn't sleep and felt all alone, Jesus was with me. But often, I seemed to forget that fact. My humanness overshadowed His presence. I was trusting that God would be loyal toward me. Of course, He was, but I may not have been loyal to Him during some of those trying times. I had to keep His presence at the forefront of my mind.

The next day was another smooth one. I was afraid to say much about the way things were going because I didn't want to jinx it. This had truly become a God experience. Each day began with a devotional and prayer. (I was using the little book given to me in that gift bag on my simulation visit, and I added another daily devotional that guided my morning thoughts.) I tried to maintain focus on my theme—James 1:2–3—throughout each day. Upon arriving home that day, I received two greeting cards. One of the cards raised the issue of "Why does God allow negative things to happen to good people?" This is probably something that many cancer patients ask in their minds. I believe that God allows negative things to happen to people so we can trust in and demonstrate faith in Him so He can draw nearer to us. Actually, we draw nearer to Him. The chorus of a song seems appropriate here:

> *Draw me close to you*
> *Never let me go*
> *I lay it all down again*
> *To hear you say that I'm your friend;*
> *You are my desire*
> *No one else will do*
> *'Cause nothing else can take your place*
> *To feel the warmth of your embrace*
> *Help me find the way*
> *Bring me back to you.*
> (Kelly Carpenter, "Draw Me Close")

Adversity gives us a chance to rely on Him. We need adversity. We need trials in our lives. Trials = JOY. It is a mindset. Instead of thinking, *What is God doing to me?* we should be thinking, *What is God doing for me?*

Just prior to my treatment session, the radiation technicians took a few pictures of me while I was lying on the table, strapped into my mask. I wanted my family and a few friends to be able to see what I was going through when I went to the cancer center. Most people do not get to see the radiation treatment area unless they are the ones receiving the treatment. It looked a bit like aliens were going to do something to my body. I found it interesting and wanted to share, and a picture is worth a thousand words, right?

Thursday and Friday of that week went okay. I was so dry on Thursday that it was almost impossible for me to swallow at all during my treatment. It was getting tougher near the end of that day's radiation treatment, but I got through it. On Friday, I had a bit of difficulty with the back of my throat; it was still quite dry. I will never take a drink of water for granted again. I was looking forward to my next chemotherapy treatment on Monday, but my lab results showed low levels in a number of areas. Therefore, I had to wait an extra week before my second chemotherapy treatment session. I had a low white blood count, low neutrophils, and more. Neutrophils are a particular white blood cell that protects the body from infection. When a person doesn't have enough neutrophils, called neutropenia, the body can't fight off bacteria, increasing the risk for many types of infection. This was of special importance to me because of my compromised immune system (a result of my leukemia many years ago). There may be merit to review Psalm 46 at this time:

> *God is our refuge and strength, an ever-present help in trouble. Therefore we will not fear, though the earth give way and the mountains fall into the heart of the sea, though its waters roar and foam and the mountains quake with their surging. There is a river whose streams make glad the city of God, the holy place where the Most High dwells. God is within her, she will not fall; God will help her at break of day. Nations are in uproar, kingdoms fall; he lifts his voice, the earth melts. The LORD Almighty is with us; the God of Jacob is our fortress. Come and see what the LORD has done, the desolations he has brought on the earth. He makes wars cease to the ends of the earth. He breaks the bow and shatters the spear; he burns the shields with fire. He says, "Be still, and know that I am God; I will be exalted*

among the nations, I will be exalted in the earth."
The LORD Almighty is with us; the God of Jacob is
our fortress.

With three weeks of my treatment (fourteen radiation sessions) completed, we were at a point where added strength was needed. Knowing God was my fortress helped me stay tough during the woes of treatment.

During the previous week, the NCAA national football championship game was played, and the NFL playoffs were underway to determine its champion. Although I am a lifelong fan of the game of football, sometimes it can be so disappointing. There are numerous fantastic athletes, many of whom seem to be greatly self-absorbed and show an "all about me" attitude. It aggravates me. And while the demonstrations of "look at me" actions go on, there is such a poor showing of basic fundamental skills (blocking and tackling) during the actual game play. Today's players can get away with this because they are such great athletes that they can make up for their lack of fundamental skills. As a former coach, it frustrates me to my bones. So as champions were being determined, I felt grateful for the true champions that were taking care of me every day. The nurses and technicians at the cancer center were my champions…where it really mattered.

By the way, during all those football games (and I watched a lot of them), I kept seeing commercials for pizza. How great would a pizza and pop be? There were other commercials for food establishments (pancakes, burgers, and specialty sandwiches). On the one hand, it was hard not to be able to load up, as was my custom during football games. Pizza may not have always been available, but the chips were always in abundance! On the other hand, it is getting easier to go without my favorite game foods…any food, really. At this point, I was not feeling hungry anymore. I didn't feel the need for food. I just wanted it! I am sure I will appreciate those foods so much more when I can have them again.

The next week could have been dubbed "sore throat" week as the pain was worse than it had ever been. It seemed to go in waves—

anything from a small tick in the back of the throat to full-throttled raw and painful burning. I had to try and remember that the pain was giving me perseverance. Although difficult, the positive mindset was a must to be successful in completing my treatments. Again, I had to remember Wooden's "Make each day your masterpiece" quote. When I thought of that quote, I also recalled the apostle Paul's instruction that I am God's masterpiece, His handiwork. Knowing that made the pain a bit more bearable.

I was enjoying the pretreatment talks with the other patients, learning about their different lives and stories. Cancer is the great equalizer—all ages, all ethnicities, both genders, etc. While some may only receive eight radiation treatments, others might be pre-scribed thirty-five radiation treatments (like me). Regardless, all of us were experiencing the basic desire to live at a time when death was a possibility. It was fun getting to know them better. Some would no longer show up because they had completed their treatments while new people filtered into the group. I always tried to be positive and encouraging. Some of the patients really needed a little lift prior to their treatments.

The Thursday of that week was a significant point in my treat-ment. It was the eighteenth radiation treatment—over halfway to the goal, on the downhill slope. There was a time when my mom turned fifty years of age. Where she was employed, there were three other ladies that worked alongside her. They were all in their thirties and gave her a little ribbing about hitting the big five-oh (fifty), making comments about being over the hill. Her reply to them was "Once you're over the hill, you pick up speed." So the press was on. I had passed the halfway mark and was going to pick up speed to my recov-ery. Surely, I knew that there would still be difficult days ahead, but the finish line was now on the horizon. Every day is a good day to have a good day. And every day holds the chance for a miracle. Well, my miracle was coming to fruition.

The month ended with my second round of chemotherapy. It was a long day. With the chemotherapy session scheduled for 8:00 a.m., our car was pulling out of the driveway a little before 7:00 a.m. The radiation treatment was scheduled for 2:10 p.m., which meant we were headed home around 3:00 p.m. Between the two sessions, I had a phone meeting with the nutritionist to talk about how my feeding regimen was going. The fatigue was overwhelming, but it was all part of the potential healing. Seeking perseverance, I turned to God's Word:

> *Let your eyes look straight ahead; fix your gaze directly before you. Give careful thought to the paths for your feet and be steadfast in all your ways.* (Proverbs 4:25–26)

> *Brothers and sisters, I do not consider myself yet to have taken hold of it. But one thing I do: Forgetting what is behind and straining toward what is ahead, I press on toward the goal to win the prize for which God has called me heavenward in Christ Jesus.* (Philippians 3:13–14)

> *Let us not become weary in doing good, for at the proper time we will reap a harvest if we do not give up.* (Galatians 6:9)

There was a bonus offering to close the month of January. The temperature climbed to sixty-six degrees! In January! In Missouri! What a gorgeous day to view as we drove home from the cancer clinic. Of course, I slept most of the way. Sleep was good. I needed it. I was at a critical juncture of my recovery. I had to face adversity, my trial. I had to persevere. I had to keep God close to me if I wanted to be at the happiest place on earth, my magic kingdom, His presence.

His presence—why is it so important? This question can be answered by looking at the work of Martin Luther. Martin Luther's work helped spread the gospel of Jesus Christ throughout the entire world. When studying if it is possible to reconcile the demands of God's law with our human inability to live up to that law, Martin

Luther, during the early 1500s, found his answer in the apostle Paul's letter to the Romans. Luther wrote,

> *In the death of Jesus Christ on the Cross, God had reconciled humanity to Himself. Christ was now the sole mediator between God and man, and forgiveness of sin and salvation are effected by God's grace alone, and are received by faith. What was required, therefore, was not a person's strict adherence to the law or the fulfillment of religious obligations, but a response of faith that accepted what God had done in the finished work of Christ. As such faith matured, it would lead to obedience based not on fear of punishment, but on love. (Foxe's Book of Martyrs, 126)*

Christ gave all He had for you and me. He suffered and gave up His life on the cross because of my sin and your sin. He rose from the dead, conquering all. Drawing nearer to His presence is where we find JOY—His presence. Nowhere else do we find true JOY, pure JOY—the JOY of eternal life.

> *Therefore, since we are surrounded by such a great cloud of witnesses, let us throw off everything that hinders and the sin that so easily entangles. And let us run with perseverance the race marked out for us, fixing our eyes on Jesus, the pioneer and perfecter of faith. For the joy set before him he endured the cross, scorning its shame, and sat down at the right hand of the throne of God. (Hebrews 12:1–2)*

> *Standing on the promises I cannot fall,*
> *List'ning every moment to the Spirit's call,*
> *Resting in my Savior as my all in all,*
> *Standing on the promises of God.*
> (Russell Carter "Standing on the Promises")

The happiest place on earth: sitting next to Keri.

CHAPTER 6

I Cannot Tell a Lie

February—what an amazing month! There are so many special days and events during our shortest month of the year: Groundhog Day, Abraham Lincoln's birthday, Valentine's Day, and George Washington's birthday. Of course, we now celebrate President's Day in lieu of Abe's and George's special days. I remember being released from school on both the twelfth and twenty-second of February for their birthdays when I was a young kid. (I never really got over the loss of both days.) There are other meaningful events during the month. It is American Heart Month, National Grapefruit Month, Potato Lovers Month, National Pet Dental Health Month, and Return Shopping Carts to the Supermarket Month, to name a few of the special things going on. Also, there is National Eat Ice Cream for Breakfast Day, National Girls and Women in Sport Day, Random Acts of Kindness Week, the Tootsie Roll's "birthday," National Organ Donor Day, National Girl Scout Cookie Weekend, World Cancer Day, plus so much more.

So let's take a moment to talk about George Washington. One of the great myths in our nation's history involves George Washington (for the longest time, I did not know it was a myth). I actually think I first heard the story as a youngster in elementary school. The story begins with George turning six years old and receiving a hatchet as a gift. He used the hatchet to hack up his father's cherry tree. His father became angry and challenged the young boy, confronting him about who harmed his tree. Showing great bravery, young George responded, "I cannot tell a lie… I did cut it with my hatchet." George's father hugged him and praised him for his honesty, claiming that his honesty was worth more than a thousand trees. Well, I cannot tell a lie…cancer sucks!

That said, treatment on the first day of February went well; the process seemed easy. Following the zapping of radiation, my wife and I met with the radiation oncologist. He said that everything "looked good." The doctor encouraged us, saying that I was making good progress and that we should be pleased with the results so far. Hearing that from the doctor made accepting the negative side effects of treatment a bit easier. Of course, I had to remember that it was God who was helping me through this trial. He took my burdens, making them tolerable for me. Psalm 55:22 reads,

> *Cast your cares* [burdens] *on the* L ORD *and he will*
> *sustain you; he will never let the righteous be shaken.*

Often, I forget to cast my burdens on my Lord. Why is that? I guess it is because I am human. But He knows that. He knows what I need even when I don't. In addition, Exodus 33:14 says,

> *The* L ORD *replied, "My Presence will go with you,*
> *and I will give you rest."*

No circumstance, trial, or situation can isolate me from God. He is always with me. I can be at rest (accept) whatever happens in life if I maintain that close relationship with God.

> *And he walks with me*
> *And he talks with me*

And he tells me I am his own
And the joy we share as we tarry there
None other has ever known. (Charles Austin Miles,
    "In the Garden")

The following day, there was no treatment because of the weather. I was a little worried about missing a treatment, but the doctor said not to worry about it. "It is better to miss a treatment day than end up with your car going into a ditch alongside the highway." It is amazing how it can be sixty-six degrees on Monday and then snow and ice on Wednesday—Missouri winter weather! I actually missed going in for treatment. I wanted to get this whole process done and over with. Face it head on, rush straight toward the challenges and trials, and not run away from the pain.

I was thinking about the snow day. There was a lot of snow dropped on us in our community. It was wet, and it was heavy. During that morning, I was sitting inside the house, reading or watching TV or working on a jigsaw puzzle while my wife shoveled the snow. She did all the work. It frustrated me to see her sling that snow shovel. That was supposed to be my job. I had shoveled the snow for years and years. I kind of liked doing it. It wasn't my job because she couldn't do it. Obviously, she could, but she shouldn't have to. Even though I was physically unable to shovel snow, I missed having the ability to do so. With the fatigue and neuropathy setting in, walking was becoming more difficult, let alone shoveling snow off the driveway and sidewalks.

Thursday went okay. The roads were clear, and treatment resumed. Things were beginning to feel automatic. It's funny—I didn't like the treatment, but I liked going to treatment. Again, I was amazed at the professionals at the cancer center. They were wonderful not only for their expertise and skills but also with the way they employed their craft. They could actually make cancer treatment pleasant. They were great!

Every Friday seemed to provide a turning point in my treatment; every Friday signaled that the end of treatment was approaching. Friday was always a good day. But this particular Friday was not so fun. My enthusiasm waned a bit. There was a lot of stuff coming up into my throat on this day—coughing, hacking, ejecting! The ejection was not an easy task because what was coming up was pretty thick and sticky. The radiation affected my salivary glands. Then the body overreacted, trying to produce saliva. It manifested itself in these ropelike strands of sticky goo that needed to be pulled out of my mouth. Ropes! That is what the doctor called those gluelike strands of yuck. As hard as I would try to spit them out, they were stubborn. I was given some special spongy swabs to wipe the ropes away. It seemed that as soon as I was able to pull most of the ropes out of my mouth, more appeared. So the cycle continued throughout the day, week, etc. But it was becoming increasingly difficult to open my mouth wide enough for those spongy swabs to work well.

Then there was the tinny taste in my mouth; it tasted like battery acid. Recall that I was unable to drink, making it difficult to wash the acrid taste out of my mouth. How is it that the radiation could kill my sense of taste, yet I was tasting battery acid? It didn't make sense to me. Of course, I didn't need to understand it. I needed to accept it and move on, not dwelling on the negative but trying to maintain a positive mindset. I may have gotten a little cocky, feeling that the treatment process was becoming simpler. Yet every time I had a good day or two, I would then experience some of the most undesirable of days.

In retrospect, I think God was trying to tell me something for the umpteenth time. Trust Him, lean on Him, and allow Him to take on my burdens. I needed to lean on Him. Like the old hymn says,

> *Leaning, leaning,*
> *Safe and secure from all alarms;*
> *Leaning, leaning,*
> *Leaning on the everlasting arms.*
> (Iris DeMent, "Leaning on the Everlasting Arms")

I needed to demonstrate confidence and faith in Him! Sure, this particular trial was painful, but God could use my adversity for His purposes, equipping me with the necessary skills or mindset to be a good example for others. Look at the life of Joseph. He faced such difficult times; he was rejected and sold into slavery by his brothers, thrown into prison and forgotten, and so much more. Yet he endured and ended up serving others, saving a great multitude of people including the brothers that sold him into slavery during the great famine. (To read about Joseph, consult chapters 37–50 of Genesis.)

Joseph's willingness to serve others provides a great example for all of us. Setting a good example—that is what I wanted to do. But that was not always the case for me. When I was an undergraduate college student, my last semester was to be spent student teaching. That meant the first two weeks of the semester was spent in the college classroom with all the other student teachers before beginning the actual student teaching experience. The cohort was made up of the group of students who had gone through the education preparation program together.

The teacher leading the student teaching cohort also happened to be my advisor in the education department. Toward the end of the first day, she announced that a sign-up sheet for making coffee was being circulated around the room. Each student was to select a day to make the morning coffee and prepare all the elements that went along with it (creamer, stir sticks, napkins, etc.). Just prior to the end of the day, our leader called on me and said, "Dennis, I see your name is not on the coffee list. Do you want to pick a day?" I replied, "No. I am not a coffee drinker." I figured that if I didn't drink any coffee, I shouldn't need to make coffee for anyone else. In hindsight, I probably should have gladly signed up for a day and cheerfully served the other students. But I didn't. After chastising me for being selfish, my advisor stated, "It sounds like someone may not be ready to student teach." Wow. Was she really going to ban me from student teaching over coffee? After class, I went to the other education instructor and told him what happened. He said, "Don't worry. I am now your new advisor. Let me take care of it." Bottom line: Not only did I student teach, but I was the first one in the cohort to secure a teaching job for the following year. Again, I should have been more gracious and taken the opportunity to serve others. Imagine, forty-two years of teaching could have been lost due to my selfish mindset. Hopefully, I am a nicer person today than I was back then.

The following week of treatment began after an infusion of gamma globulin on Monday, a procedure I had been going through for years. When I had leukemia numerous years ago, the chemotherapy killed all the "bad stuff" in me. When that occurred, the chemotherapy also killed the "good stuff." Usually, the good stuff was supposed to recover, and a person would be back to normal. In my case, all the good stuff did not recover. So I have been lacking a certain element that helps fight off infection. Every four weeks, I am infused with what I refer to as super juice. Once, I was in the hospital because of what was called disseminated shingles. (This was my third bout with shingles.) I wasn't feeling well and had a few good-sized black spots on my hand. While in the hospital, the black spots started to appear on my legs. One day, during the typical doctor rounds, one of the rotating doctors with a specialty in infectious diseases had a feeling I was missing something. He was the one that diagnosed my need for the monthly infusions. I remember asking him how long I would need to receive the infusions. His response was "How long do you want to live?" When it comes to life illnesses, the good doctors do not mess around. So every four weeks, I sit in a chair for about four hours, having this life-changing substance pushed into my veins.

After spending four hours being infused in one hospital, I left to go to the cancer center for my radiation treatment. It may have been one of the best zapping sessions up to that point. At first it was a little uncomfortable; when they snapped me onto the radiation table, there was some discomfort, but I had learned that sometimes a small change of position alleviated the irritable aches. So a little shift of my head and neck, a relaxing of the shoulders, and a restful mindset made it okay. No discomfort equals a quick and easy treatment session. Psalm 46:10 tells us,

Be still, and know that I am God.

Sometimes, just being still allows the patient to resettle, relax, and rest during a session. Going into that restful mindset allowed me to focus on God's presence. Lying on the radiation table, I tried to center my thoughts on God's gifts—all the blessings I had received over the years. It made treatment easier to deal with. Knowing who God is and reflecting on His love for me (us) can lead to true rest.

Coincidently, the emphasis of that morning's devotional was to "rest in the peace of Christ." How often do we purposefully rest? Not take a nap! View the situation we are in, connect with Christ through prayer, and then let go of the hard parts of life. Matthew 11:28 reads,

> *Come to me, all you who are weary and burdened,*
> *and I will give you rest.*

Jesus tells us to bring our burdens to Him. He will take our pain and rest it on His shoulders. Does it still hurt? Yes, maybe, but we can share our pain with Christ. He can ease the pain just enough for us to feel His peace. Then we can rest.

Think about that for a moment. When do we rest in the arms of Jesus Christ? If He tells us to do something (e.g., bring our burdens to Him), we should hold Him accountable! Demonstrate faith and trust in Him. Give Him our pain. Give Him our woes. Give Him our lives!

> *For our light and momentary troubles are achieving*
> *for us an eternal glory that far outweighs them all.*
> *So we fix our eyes not on what is seen, but on what*
> *is unseen, since what is seen is temporary, but what*
> *is unseen is eternal.* (2 Corinthians 4:17–18)

Psalm 42:5 tells us to put our hope in God. It isn't like "I hope it doesn't rain," where we are not sure of the outcome. Hope in Christ is a sure thing!

> *Why, my soul, are you downcast? Why so disturbed*
> *within me? Put your hope in God, for I will yet*
> *praise him, my Savior and my God.* (Psalm 42:5)

When the apostle Paul tells us to be joyful in hope, it is a hope with assurance. That assurance should give us all the JOY we can handle.

> *Be joyful in hope, patient in affliction, faithful in prayer.* (Romans 12:12)

The next day's treatment included prayer and communion with God. It went well, almost easy. It still wiped me out (fatigue), but I continued to struggle sleeping at night. How could I be so tired and not be able to sleep? My body was going through a lot. The radiation and chemotherapy treatments could be harsh. When we met with the doctor after my radiation session on this day, he was again pleased with my progress: "Everything seems to be going well." In our meeting, he answered many of our questions. One question was "How do we know if the treatment is working?" Once the treatments were completed, we could still be waiting for months to know if they worked. A CT scan would be scheduled to see if my throat was clear of any foreign mass. We were also told that the radiation would continue to impact the body long after the treatments ended.

The doctor was pleased with my weight even though I was down a bit. He said that the body was working overtime, using a lot of energy to respond to the treatments. I had been bumped up to six cartons of "food," hoping to increase or at least maintain my weight. Each carton contained a little over eight ounces of fluid nutrition equaling 375 calories. Although it may not sound like much, it was difficult to consume six cartons even though they were spread over the entire day. Once I complete the treatment and recover from its aftereffects, I hope to begin trying to eat real food again, starting with mashed potatoes, pudding, Cream of Wheat, and other soft foods to retrain the swallowing muscles of my throat. I was told I would have to learn how to swallow food safely again. I remember thinking, *How do you to learn to swallow?* I thought it was one of those things that you just did. You know…just do it.

The next day was significant. After my radiation session, we were down to single digits of treatments remaining—the last nine radiation treatments—sprinting to the end. Although I could get excited to be done, there would still be work to do once the treatments ended. I wondered how long it would take for my throat to recover. (As it turns out, I later learned that it usually takes eighteen to twenty-four months to completely recover to "normal" status.) I wondered if the treatments were working. It still hurt, and interestingly, the left side of my throat hurt more than the right side sometimes. Yet the cancer was on the right side. I didn't understand that. The ropes had also increased, making it difficult to clear my mouth. Gargling had become more difficult. I still tried to do it, but it was bothersome. Did I say it hurt? Yeah, it hurt a lot.

Earlier in the day, I had an appointment with my regular primary care provider. I had been going to this doctor for quite some time. Today he had lots of questions about my treatment and how he might assist in my recovery. Between my two oncologists, the ENT (ear, nose, and throat) specialist, the pulmonologist, and the infectious disease specialist, it was amazing that we were all on the same page. At least I thought we were. There may have been a difference of opinion here and there, but for the most part, all were headed in the same direction. My regular doctor may have been a bit out of the loop, but he cared and tried to be up on what was happening to me.

The last two days of the week were uneventful. It still hurt, and it still tasted like battery acid. But I couldn't complain. I woke up that day, and if I wake up, it is a good day! I tried to nap here and there. Actually, I didn't need to try. When I watched television, I would periodically nod off for a bit. Nighttime sleep was still difficult, though. But it could have been a whole lot worse. GRATITUDE! I was trying to show the nurses and technicians how much I appreciated them. I brought a gift for my oncologists to demonstrate my gratitude for their efforts. They were surprised but pleased to receive the small token of my esteem (a book about a miraculous story involving a premature baby and the doctors and nurses that saved that baby's life).

Our in-laws came by and brought me flowers and a card. On the weekend, the deacons at my church were having a breakfast and then coming by as part of a prayer walk. So many people had sent me cards and texts, most offering prayers on my behalf, and offered to help in many ways. On one snowy day, a couple of really good friends picked us up in their truck and drove Keri and me to the cancer center for my treatment. We probably would have had to skip another day if we were driving ourselves, but our friends' truck could easily handle the roads during poor weather. They wouldn't even allow us to pay to refill their gas tank with fuel. This same couple called another time and said, "We'll be driving you to the cancer center on Friday." Amid our meager objections telling them it wasn't necessary, they told us there was no discussion to be had. They were driving us. Those are good friends; they delivered JOY that day! All these examples of the kindness, care, and love brought me great JOY.

The Super Bowl was coming that weekend. Normally, that would require a special trip to the store to load up on chips and pop (and other food and snacks) for the game. Not this year. Again, I couldn't complain. I was happy to be alive and well enough to watch the game. Today's devotion focused on JOY, my theme for this entire process. Was I considering the JOY to be found in my trial? I had to continually keep my mind focused on JOY as the best option. We always have choices in life. I could choose to be negative and grouchy, or I could remember that the Creator of the universe had my back. That should always bring me JOY!

> *The Lord is my shepherd, I lack nothing. He makes me lie down in green pastures, he leads me beside quiet waters, he refreshes my soul. He guides me along the right paths for his name's sake. Even though I walk through the darkest valley, I will fear no evil, for you are with me; your rod and your staff they comfort me. You prepare a table before me in the presence of my enemies. You anoint my head with oil; my cup overflows. Surely your goodness and love will follow me all the days of my life, and I will dwell in the house of the Lord forever. (Psalm 23)*

Give thanks with a grateful heart
Give thanks to the Holy One
Give thanks because He's given
Jesus Christ, His Son.

And now let the weak say, "I am strong"
Let the poor say, "I am rich"
Because of what the Lord has done for us.
(Henry Smith, "Give Thanks with a Grateful
     Heart")

Cancer sucks! At times, the medication made me a bit incoherent.

CHAPTER 7

Happy Valentine's Day

Valentine's Day is a time to express our love for others. I have always enjoyed creating gifts for the family on Valentine's Day. Chocolate was always a part of the celebration of my love for them. And of course, I would sample the goods. Even in present day, I send gifts to the kids even though they are grown and out of the house. I used to mail a sweet package to my oldest son's work just to embarrass him a little. But what it really did was show others that worked around him that his parents still loved him. The kids could probably predict that there would always be a little something in their mailboxes a few days before the love holiday. I still usually sample, although not this year.

Here is a different kind of love story for Valentine's Day. For a while, I was a track-and-field coach. I attended a conference for coaches where successful or elite coaches shared techniques with other coaches. As a young coach, I was interested in attending a session offered by a former Olympic coach. This coach was particularly strong in the jumps—high jump, long jump, and triple jump. Since that was part of my responsibility, I went, hoping to learn about coaching jumpers; but instead, I learned an amazing life lesson.

This coach, let's call him Jim, was an elite coach known for his athletes' successes. Because of his notoriety, Jim was often asked to speak in front of others. One day, a woman called him on the phone and asked if he would coach her son for an upcoming Special Olympics track meet. Jim told her he was quite busy and didn't know if he could make the time to coach her son. A few days later, the woman called up the coach a second time. She told him it would mean a lot to her son and that if Jim participated in the Special Olympics track meet, it might generate more interest because of his past Olympic successes. Jim told the woman he would give it some thought. What if this kid didn't perform well? What would people think of him? He was concerned that being seen working with such low-level athletes might harm his reputation as an elite Olympic coach. A couple of days later, Jim received yet another phone call from the determined mother. Jim relented and agreed to coach the young boy.

That afternoon, when Jim drove home, he was met at the base of his driveway by this young special needs boy. The boy was jumping up and down, yelling, "Hey, Coach, I'm ready!" Jim kept driving. The driveway was quite steep, but as Jim drove up the driveway, he saw the boy chasing after him in the rearview mirror. He felt a bit embarrassed. The next day, the same thing occurred. And the next day, the same episode took place. Finally, Jim made arrangements with the boy's mother to meet at the local track. The boy was not a very good runner, but Jim put in his time and coached the boy.

At the Special Olympics track meet, Jim saw that each runner had a person that would be on the track to encourage the runners. These encouragers would meet the runners at the finish line, give them a hug, and congratulate them on their race. Prior to the boy's race, the meet was halted to introduce Jim as an elite Olympic coach and the coach of this young boy. Jim started getting nervous. Of all the big, high-level meets Jim had coached in, he never felt this kind of anxiousness about a race or event. He took his place at the finish line and looked down at the boy, who was getting ready to begin the race. At the sound of the starter's pistol, the runners were off. The boy began running, weaving in and out of his lane and quickly falling behind all the other runners. *Oh no,* thought Jim. He was so embarrassed that his "protégé" was performing so badly. As the boy neared the finish line, well behind all the other runners, he fell into the arms of his coach and uttered, "I did it, Daddy!"

The applause was astounding to Jim. He realized that how the boy placed in the race was not really important. He felt such JOY, knowing that he had spent a little time with the boy. Yes, the woman who hounded Jim to coach her son was his wife. The boy who finished last in the race was his son. And he never felt better about any track event in his life. As he finished his talk, Coach Jim told the audience that at every speaking engagement after that moment, he agreed to appear only if he was allowed to tell this story. He wanted to spread the word not only about the Special Olympics but also about the love of participation by the athletes and the love between a dad and his son. This is not a typical Valentine's Day love story, but it goes straight to the heart of the matter: love always wins! Love is where we can find JOY!

> *Jesus said, "Let the little children come to me, and do not hinder them, for the kingdom of heaven belongs to such as these."* (Matthew 19:14)

> *Dear children, let us not love with words or speech but with actions and in truth.* (1 John 3:18)

As I entered or left the cancer center, I saw many different people, each with their own story. Did they have a love celebration for Valentine's Day? I wondered if they had support like I did. Were they alone? Were they scared? Cancer can be such an imposing foe, yet Jesus was bearing the brunt for me spiritually, emotionally, and even physically. What about the others I saw? Were they aware that Christ could ease their pain? I was sure many of them were afraid and anxious about how to approach their treatment. Adversity can be painful, and each person may suffer different levels of discomfort. There is no JOY for them in their pain, their trial. Recall that my theme for treatment came from James 1:2–3, which says we should consider trials as pure JOY and that the testing of our faith produces perseverance. In chapter 5 of his letter to the Romans, the apostle Paul tells us that suffering produces perseverance, perseverance builds character, and character leads to hope. James 1:4 states,

> *Let perseverance finish its work so that you may be mature and complete, not lacking anything.*

Perseverance seems to be a by-product of our adversity. So while we are sometimes hit in the face with trials, we should be joyful, knowing that we are in the process of gaining perseverance. (Note: when the Bible repeats itself, we should take note—this is important—that it is being repeated for my [our] edification.) For us to be totally mature and complete, we need to persevere through troublesome times. That is one of the outcomes of God's love for us. Many may not be aware of this, but God is a permanent resident at the cancer center. We can celebrate His love, knowing that He cares for us. He is with us as we ride out the trials we face. That is why I occasionally said a silent prayer for those I would see at the cancer center.

I remember the first few months of my treatment during my leukemia days. Every single time I went to the cancer center, I saw a little old lady, a grand collection of wrinkles. She was short and quite thin. Actually, she was skinny to the point where I wondered how she supported herself. She also used a walker to slowly move around. It seemed like she must have lived at the cancer center; she was always there. Although at first, it was a passing notice of this small "bag of bones," this lady soon became an inspiration to me. There I was, a tough former football coach, and I was acquiring inspiration from this little old lady, this little "bag of bones." She was a fighter! This diminutive veteran warrior added to my perseverance; it was an "if she can make it, I can make it" kind of thing. Anyway, I am thankful for her being there. It gave me a broader perspective of the other patients during my second "tour of duty" at the cancer center.

On this Valentine's Day, I did not receive any chocolate, but I did get a dose of radiation. After a long weekend of coughing up lots of goo, I was not looking forward to lying on the radiation table (being flat seemed to prompt an increase in coughing and goo production). But the radiation technicians were their usual kind selves, going out of their way to assist me through the difficult process. I thought about bringing them some chocolate treats but didn't know who to include and who not to include. Where would I draw the line, right? The technicians, the nurses, the doctors, the receptionists…there would have been too many; and I didn't want to leave anyone out. So I gave the technicians a more direct "thank you" for all they were doing for me. They knew how much I appreciated them on this Valentine's Day.

My Valentine's Day treatment did not go easy. The soreness in my throat didn't seem to want to go away, swallowing still ached, the goo almost choked me, and the fatigue was ever present. That morning, my devotion for the day was about Christ being with me. I heard it, read it, and prayed it many times over the previous six weeks; but my humanness seemed intent on failure. In my humanity, I was weak, and the discomfort sometimes overcame the fact that Christ was with me. Isaiah 41:13 reads,

> *For I am the LORD your God who takes hold of your right Hand and says to you, Do not fear; I will help you.*

In addition, Psalm 48:14 says,

> *For this God is our God for ever and ever; he will be our guide even to the end.*

These verses (and so many others) told me I had a guide, friend, and Savior who would never let me down. Still, sometimes I had to stop, pray, and ask God to keep me focused on the fact that I was being carried by my Lord. That should elevate me above the weakness I displayed, but again, I am human. I should have rejoiced in knowing that I am God's child. It is worth noting that 2 Corinthians 12:9–10 says that I can boast about my weaknesses and delight in weaknesses, insults, hardships, persecutions, and difficulties. For when I am weak, then I am strong. His strength shines when I am weak. His grace is sufficient for me. So if I fail, all I need to do is look to Him for help. He makes me strong.

The next day, Tuesday, was a blockbuster! I realized that after this treatment session, there would only be five sessions left. The light at the end of the tunnel was shining brighter. There was a little bit more excitement than usual. Although my throat sometimes screamed its displeasure with me, it seemed to ease a bit today. It would come and go. With the treatment going surprisingly well, I was in a pretty good mood. The day's treatment finished well, and the end of all treatments seemed just around the corner. I knew that things were going to get better.

On Wednesday of that week, there was no treatment. It was cancelled because of the weather. The fact that there were only two days missed because of inclement weather in January and February in Missouri was astounding. I had started running a fever, and one of the nurses returned my wife's telephone call to check up on me. The temperature wasn't drastically high, but my wife was concerned because my body was in a weakened state. The next day, Thursday, all went fine. As we were leaving, the radiation nurse that took care of me most of the time and the one that returned my wife's call said, "I'm praying for you." This was such a short statement, but it meant so much. I gave her a "thank you" but later wished I had said more. It was nice to know that she was pulling for me.

Our friends insisted on driving us to the cancer center for Friday's treatment as another storm was possible. Even though we could have probably driven ourselves, this nice couple spent an hour driving us to the cancer center, then sat in their car while my treatment took place; and then they spent another hour driving us home. And once again, they wouldn't take any money for gas! They told us, "Anytime you need a ride, give us a call." This was a wonderful example of the support we received from friends.

> *A friend loves at all times, and a brother is born for
> a time of adversity.* (Proverbs 17:17)

My command is this: Love each other as I have loved you. Greater love has no one than this: to lay down one's life for one's friends. (John 15:12–13)

Now these friends were not going to die for us, but they went out of their way to assist us. It should be noted that driving in inclement weather can prove to be a bit dangerous. In this case, the roads were pretty clear. Where there was any residual snow on the roads, the truck had no problems keeping us on a straight path.

There was a bit of a buzz going on in my head as I entered the final week of my treatments. The buzz was created by the excitement of completing the treatment process. Also, although I was almost done, I still had questions that really couldn't be answered, like "Were the treatments working?" "Was I going to be cured?" "Was there anything I could do to keep the cancer from coming back?" and much more. My final chemotherapy treatment was moved for the second time; I was supposed to receive the treatment the previous Monday, but it was moved to this Monday and was then rescheduled again to the upcoming Wednesday…maybe. One of the oncologists was concerned about my blood levels; if certain elements of my blood were too low, treatment would be withheld. I actually had a brief hospital stay toward the end of my treatments when my blood numbers were so low. But if anther blood test showed improved numbers, Wednesday would be my last day. The doctor also ordered a chest x-ray to rule out pneumonia.

On Monday, I had to halt the radiation treatment for the second time in my overall treatment experience. Out of the blue, I could not breathe. When I raised my hand during the administration of the radiation, I was a little surprised at how quickly the technicians responded. That was greatly appreciated. They readjusted the mask, and we finished the treatment. I didn't like stopping the treatment, but I couldn't not stop it. When you can't breathe, nothing else matters. One of the technicians responded to my "I'm sorry" with "Don't worry about it, hon. If we have to stop, we stop. If we have to reschedule the session, we will. No pressure from us." She made it clear that the treatment was about ME. The treatment was an important part of my recovery, but it was not at the top of the list of priorities. I was.

That morning's devotional had been about drawing nearer to God. I was not sure if I was to draw nearer to God or if He would draw nearer to me. As it turns out, both were correct. James 4:8 states,

> *Come near to God and he will come near to you.*
> *Wash your hands, you sinners, and purify your*
> *hearts, you double-minded.*

Although God is always with me (and you), as we draw nearer to Him, He reciprocates. Maybe He makes His presence known to us in ways we don't expect. If the Bible says it, I believe it! Two verses later, it reads,

> *Humble yourselves before the Lord, and he will lift*
> *you up.* (James 4:10)

If I wanted to draw nearer to God, I had to have a humble heart. It was my hope that this was the case, but having a humble heart is an everyday thing, an every-moment thing. We are never done being humble before our God. It is a choice we make with every tick of the clock. Hebrews 10:22 tells us,

> *[L]et us draw near to God with a sincere heart and*
> *with the full assurance that faith brings, having our*
> *hearts sprinkled to cleanse us from a guilty conscience*
> *and having our bodies washed with pure water.*

For some reason, I expected a difficult treatment for the penultimate radiation session. Therefore, I prepared myself a little more than normal. I prayed more and held hands with Jesus as I entered the radiation chamber. As a result, Jesus carried me through the entire way. I was so relaxed that I almost fell asleep. There were no issues on that next-to-last day of treatment. Breathing was easy, there was no excessive soreness in my throat, and time flew by. I almost floated out of the radiation room. As always, one of the technicians walked me to the door that led to the reception area of the clinic and gave me a "Let's get excited for tomorrow," knowing it was to be my last radiation treatment.

The last day had arrived! My blood work allowed me to receive my final chemotherapy medicine. I was in one of the recliners for about four hours. I tried to read, but the excitement was getting the best of me. Also, I couldn't concentrate very well—probably a side effect of oxycodone, which made reading a bit difficult. I tried working a crossword puzzle, but my hand was creating scribbles. That was okay with me; nothing was going to curb my enthusiasm on the last day. Once the chemotherapy was over, I practically skipped down the hall to the radiation section of the building.

The radiation seemed to go pretty well. Then all of a sudden, I had to take a "barf break." I hadn't had much of that. Some people experience extreme nausea or diarrhea because of chemotherapy or radiation treatments. Most of my ejections had been the ropelike mucous structures in the back of my throat. I didn't really throw them up, but it felt like vomiting was eminent. The technician brought me a waste basket and said, "Feel free to fill 'er up." After my little barf fest, I apologized for the hassle. Again, the technician was so kind, saying, "It happens all the time. No worries."

DONE! Most people have seen (or heard) cancer patients ring that bell at the conclusion of their treatments. There is usually clapping and cheering along with well wishes. I didn't want (or need) to ring any bell. Intrinsically, I felt great about the accomplishment of completing my treatments; I didn't need the bell. The radiation nurses and technicians provided me with a completion certificate, which they all signed. The certificate included kind and encouraging words from all of them. It felt so good to walk out of the building when all my treatments were complete.

I had made it—DONE! I had been so impressed with the oncologists, nurses, and technicians that took care of me. But I must acknowledge the work of the Great Physician. Jesus healed people wherever He went. John 6:2 records this fact:

> *[A]nd a great crowd of people followed him because they saw the signs he had performed by healing the sick.*

His power was supernatural (and it still is). Some people realized this because they had seen Him perform His miracles. One woman believed so fervently that she felt that all she had to do was touch His robe, and she would be healed.

> *And a woman was there who had been subject to bleeding for twelve years. She had suffered a great deal under the care of many doctors and had spent all she had, yet instead of getting better she grew worse. When she heard about Jesus, she came up behind him in the crowd and touched his cloak, because she thought, "If I just touch his clothes, I will be healed." Immediately her bleeding stopped and she felt in her body that she was freed from her suffering."* (Mark 5:25–29)

The woman was correct. All she needed was faith in Christ, and He would know her heart and heal her. Do we believe in Jesus's power today? What truly heals us? Is it the chemotherapy or the radiation? Or is it quite possibly the grace and mercy lavished on us from our heavenly Father?

> *Then the woman, knowing what had happened to her, came and fell at his feet and, trembling with fear, told him the whole truth. He said to her, "Daughter, your faith has healed you. Go in peace and be freed from your suffering."* (Mark 5:33–34)

In addition, Jesus not only heals our physical infirmities, but He is also able to (and does) heal our broken hearts. When we are out of step with His will and shut Him out of our lives, our hearts break because we are missing His perfect love. Mark 2:17 expresses to us,

On hearing this, Jesus said to them, "It is not the healthy who need a doctor, but the sick. I have not come to call the righteous, but sinners."

When we consider the concept of love, most people think of Hollywood's version of love. They have this picture in their minds of sunny days, flowers, passionate kisses, and finding the perfect partner by bumping into a person while rounding the corner of the sidewalk. They think of Valentine's Day love. There is nothing wrong with Valentine's Day love. It just isn't as powerful as the perfect, sacrificial love Jesus offers us.

Do to others as you would have them do to you. "If you love those who love you, what credit is that to you? Even sinners love those who love them. And if you do good to those who are good to you, what credit is that to you? Even sinners do that. And if you lend to those from whom you expect repayment, what credit is that to you? Even sinners lend to sinners, expecting to be repaid in full. But love your enemies, do good to them, and lend to them without expecting to get anything back. Then your reward will be great, and you will be children of the Most High, because he is kind to the ungrateful and wicked." (Luke 6:31–35)

If you keep my commands, you will remain in my love, just as I have kept my Father's commands and remain in his love. I have told you this so that my joy may be in you and that your joy may be complete. My command is this: Love each other as I have loved

you. Greater love has no one than this: to lay down one's life for one's friends. (John 15:10–13)

Give thanks to the Lord, our God and King
His love endures forever
For He is good, He is above all things
His love endures forever…

From the rising to the setting sun
His love endures forever.
And by the grace of God, we will carry on
His love endures forever. (Chris Tomlin, "Forever")

The certificates indicate my radiation treatment was complete.

CHAPTER 8

The Boys of Summer

The Boys of Summer is a nonfiction book about baseball that was published in 1972. Primarily, the book was about part of the history of the storied Brooklyn Dodgers, and it includes their 1955 World Series championship. The book includes a look at the lives of some of the players on that team: Pee Wee Reese, Gil Hodges, Roy Campanella, Duke Snider, Jackie Robinson, and others. (The Dodgers is the team that broke the color barrier with Jackie Robinson.) Fans of the old-time Brooklyn Dodgers think of this time as the golden age of baseball. The team's name came from the pedestrians in Brooklyn who "dodged" the streetcars in the city. The Dodgers were also called the Bums, a nickname given to the team by a cartoonist in the 1930s. The players were sometimes referred to as Dem Bums.

Prior to the 1958 season, those bums (the Dodgers) were relocated to Los Angeles. Like many Southern California kids, I grew up a fan of the Los Angeles Dodgers. As a youngster, I played Little League baseball. One of my friends (Kevin) and I used to play one-on-one baseball in the front yard at my house with a Wiffle ball and bat. I would always pretend to be the Dodgers, while Kevin was always the Cardinals. We knew all the players and pretended to be those professional baseball players while we played our games. At the time, I did not even know about the Brooklyn Dodgers. I learned more about the history of the team when I was older and had an interest in sport history. So Kevin and I were boys of summer—and nobody called us bums!

My treatments were done! So why was I back at the cancer center two days after treatment ended? One of the oncologists wanted another blood test. Simple, really—a quick in and out. On the drive to the cancer center, I was mulling questions over in my head. "When does the pain go away?" "When do I know if the treatment worked?" "Will the cancer come back?" "If the cancer was found on the right side of my throat, why does the left side of my throat hurt so much?" and "When will I be able to swallow and eat real food again?"—all these questions had already been asked, but the answers were not so clear.

I was told I could anticipate the pain to begin to subside in seven to ten days. In about two to three months, I was scheduled to have a CT scan, which is like a glorified x-ray, on my neck and chest. Officially called computed tomography, a CT scan combines the use of x-rays and computer technology to create images of the inside of the body. The scan should tell the doctor if there is anything in the body that shouldn't be there. A clean scan would mean no tumor. My return to eating food would depend on how my body recovered from the treatment. The ability to swallow was greatly affected, and regaining the ability to eat real food varies from person to person. The radiation was beamed in the head and neck area, which can cause pain and other issues in the surrounding areas. (As it turned out, it would be quite a while before food made its way back into my life.) "Be patient," I was told.

Therefore, as God's chosen people, holy and dearly loved, clothe yourselves with compassion, kindness, humility, gentleness and patience. (Colossians 3:12)

Just because patience is listed last in that Bible verse does not diminish its importance. After going through seven weeks of radiation treatment, it was a bit difficult to be patient. That said, there was no other option. I had to wait. Coincidently, the fruits of the Spirit in Galatians 5:22–23 reads,

> *But the fruit of the Spirit is love, joy, peace, for-*
> *bearance, kindness, goodness, faithfulness, gentleness*
> *and self-control. Against such things there is no law.*

Sometimes people use *forbearance* interchangeably with *patience*, but it is more than that. Forbearance is a purposeful willingness to be patient, put up with disagreeable things, and not retaliate when someone wrongs you. Interestingly, in the Galatians passage, *forbearance* is wrapped between *peace* and *kindness*. It seems appropriate to think that to be patient, we must exude a peaceful and kind nature. Patience is also used in one of the Bible's often-quoted passages from 1 Corinthians:

> *Love is patient, love is kind. It does not envy, it does*
> *not boast, it is not proud. It does not dishonor oth-*
> *ers, it is not self-seeking, it is not easily angered, it*
> *keeps no record of wrongs. (1 Corinthians 13:4–5)*

When in the midst of pain and affliction, it may be difficult to demonstrate patience, but patience is something that God wants and expects from us. I had to ask God for help in being patient with my body.

A few days into the recovery phase, the ropes were still prevalent in my mouth, and the perpetual sore throat was still present. I was a bit concerned as I dropped five pounds in the week following treatment, but my body was working hard to heal itself. I tried to keep up with the nutrition plan to monitor my weight. I was also gargling a salt-and-baking-soda solution, taking my medications, and pushing forward with my recovery.

Nine days after my treatment ended, I didn't know what to expect as I went to my next doctor appointment. Not much really happened; it was just a follow-up to see how I was doing. The following Monday, I had my regularly scheduled infusion; and the next day, I had a fever. The oncologist explained the low numbers from my blood work and directed us to go directly to the hospital. It was a collective decision between the medical oncologist and the radiation oncologist. There was a fear I had developed an infection of some kind. In the old days, they would have shot me up with some antibiotics, and a few days later I would be fine. With my compromised immune system, the doctors didn't want to take any chances. So I spent two days in the hospital—definitely not a vacation.

Recall that my plan was to see JOY in this experience. How could God produce JOY from cancer treatments? I tried to listen to God, hear His teaching, and find the JOY. If I sat back and waited for JOY to find me, nothing would happen. Wait, Jesus Christ is JOY. So if I am in His presence, there is JOY in an abundance. I just needed to find it. In my weakness, it was a constant battle. The morning devotionals were helpful as they kept me connected with Christ. I truly tried to seek His presence, listen to Him, and let Him bless me. He sure did!

The two weeks following my admittance into the hospital were hard. It was strongly suggested that I stay somewhat quarantined because of my compromised immune system. I did very little; I just stayed at home. I didn't go anywhere. I had no doctor appointments or treatments. It was the safe thing to do. But the boredom of recovery was difficult. Normally, watching television, reading, and doing jigsaw puzzles was fine; but the medication I was taking made concentration problematic. My routine was fairly strict: four feedings and five waterings a day. My wife took some time away from her school job during the spring to take care of me (she was a speech-language pathologist at an elementary school).

It seemed that the pain had localized to my jaw and right behind my right ear. I was coughing up less gunk, and there were fewer ropes. The swallowing attempt was coming soon. I was a bit fearful of that. I wondered how much it would hurt, and I questioned whether I would be able to swallow effectively. Sleep was still difficult. Much of my sleeping was done in the recliner. I used to joke about doing two to three miles a day in the recliner. Lying flat on the bed caused too much coughing. I thought that if I could sleep better, I might recover quicker. However, I wasn't going to push it too much; slow and steady wins the race, right? This was to be a marathon, not a sprint. But I will finish this race! Recall Hebrews 12:1, which says,

> *Therefore, since we are surrounded by so great a cloud of witnesses, let us also lay aside every weight, and sin which clings so closely, and let us run with endurance the race that is set before us.*

My next oncology appointment went well. It started with blood work. The doctor was pleased with my lab work. She also indicated that my immune history might be the cause for a longer recovery. It was a good feeling, walking out of the cancer center following a positive appointment. When the doctors were pleased, everything else seemed just a bit easier, lighter.

Of course, two days later would find me in the midst of a really rough day. I had severe pain in my face and jaw. I had developed a side effect called trismus. Trismus is a spasm in the jaw muscle that causes it to lock in place, often referred to as lock jaw. Once I started going to occupational therapy, the therapist measured my jaw opening at only 0.3 centimeters. With many massaging and stretching exercises, I was eventually able to use a baby toothbrush meant for two-year-old children.

I couldn't get enough oxycodone to keep the pain in my cheeks and jaw in check. It was frustrating not being able to reduce the pain. Also, there was a lot of swelling in my face and neck. However, I did get some sleep during the day. One difficult day turned into a couple of rough weeks. Without any doctor appointments eminent, I had to grin and bear it. The facial swelling had become quite painful, and the medication didn't seem to help much. We sent a picture of my face to the radiation oncologist. He said it was lymphedema. Lymphedema is when swelling occurs because fluid that is usually drained through the body's lymphatic system builds up. The doctor also told us that it was quite normal. I kept hearing that: "Things are normal, hang in there." It's a nice way to say, "Be patient." My throat was still pretty sore. I was trying to swallow once in a while. Dry swallows seemed to be better than trying to swallow something, even water. I had a fear of swallowing anything because of the potential of acquiring aspiration pneumonia, so I kept my swallowing to the dry swallows—nothing in my mouth that could go down the wrong tube.

I was really struggling to sleep at night. I thought I needed to pray more as the evening wound down, not only to pray more but to pray better. The intent was to commune with God. But sometimes my mind seemed to wander during my prayers. The difficulty to focus and concentrate appeared to infiltrate my prayer life. I hoped I was not being offensive to God in my feeble prayer life. I thought about coming up with a sleep prayer, but that never happened. When I was at a loss, I would think of how Jesus taught His disciples to pray:

> *This, then, is how you should pray: "Our Father in heaven, hallowed be your name, your kingdom come, your will be done, on earth as it is in heaven. Give us today our daily bread. And forgive us our debts, as we also have forgiven our debtors. And lead us not into temptation, but deliver us from the evil one."* (Matthew 6:9–13)

Just prior to that, Jesus told the disciples that God knows what we need before we even ask.

> *Do not be like them, for your Father knows what you need before you ask him.* (Matthew 6:8)

This verse was a comfort to me. It took the pressure off praying that perfect prayer. As a matter of fact, once in a while, I would pray, "Lord, You know what I need. Please take care of me." He understands our human weakness. Of course, He does. He made us.

Just like those Dodgers and Little Leaguers all across the country who were getting ready to play their games during the summer, as the midsummer approached, my feeling was that this would be a season of strong recovery. I expected it. I had completed my treatments and was doing all that the doctors told me to do. It didn't take long before my positive expectations were once again thrashed.

One night near the end of April, I couldn't sleep; so I got up from bed, went into our book room, and was in the recliner, reading. All of a sudden, I began to cough up blood—lots of it! I called to my wife, and she helped me up and into the car. Off we dashed to the emergency room.

The emergency team tried to get my symptoms under control. Eventually, they got me stabilized, but they felt it was crucial that they send me to a larger hospital, one that could handle my issues. They wanted to send me by way of a helicopter. But it was a stormy night, so the helicopter was a no-go. That meant I would experience my first-ever ride in an ambulance. The emergency team called a hospital in Kansas City, but they wouldn't take me because I couldn't be intubated because of my trismus. Another hospital was called, and they accepted me. It took the ambulance almost an hour to reach the hospital. Not thirty minutes after arriving, they decided to call the hospital in Kansas City again; but for some reason, the hospital agreed to take me this time. I was put into another ambulance that took me to a major hospital in Kansas City.

At the hospital, the ear, nose, and throat doctor (ENT) performed a tracheostomy. He surgically created an opening through the neck into the trachea (windpipe). A tube (trach) was placed through the opening to provide an airway and to remove secretions from the lungs. It was a safety issue. In case the need ever arose, I was unable to be intubated because of my trismus, which was caused by the radiation. This particular trach was "cuffed" (a balloon-like feature is attached to the tube and helps protect the airway). Breathing was done through the tracheostomy tube instead of the nose and mouth. The term *tracheotomy* refers to the incision into the trachea (windpipe) that forms a temporary or permanent opening, which is called a tracheostomy. There is *tracheotomy* and *tracheostomy*; they are different, but the terms are often used interchangeably.

A bleeding ulcer was found in the back of my throat—a symptom of the radiation. I couldn't do much of anything other than lie in bed. I couldn't even talk. The trach made it impossible for me to speak at all. So for a number of days, I lay in bed, doing nothing. To communicate with the doctors, nurses, and family, I had to write things on a notepad. After four days, I was sent home. Just prior to going home, the doctor exchanged my trach tube for a different kind of trach. This one had a speaking valve, which allowed me to communicate with others. My daughter had flown in from Boston to support me and help take care of me. She ended up staying for two months. Her help was indescribable.

My return home lasted one day. A home health nurse came to our house the following day and didn't like the way I looked. I had a fever, my oxygen level was pretty low, and my heart rate was quite high. So on the advice of the home health nurse, I was awarded another ambulance ride back to the medical center in Kansas City. At the hospital, my temperature climbed up to 104 degrees, and my heart was racing. I ended up with pneumonia and stayed in the hospital for another five days. Later, I learned about something called *pseudomonas aeruginosa*, which is a common cause of hospital-acquired pneumonia. This is a frequent and severe cause of hospital-acquired infections, particularly in patients that are immunocompromised (that's me!). My wife and daughter spent most of that time in the hospital, by my side. The trach tube was changed yet again to a cuffed version to help prevent aspiration—but no speaking valve. So when I was sent home, I spent the next couple of weeks unable to talk to my wife or daughter unless I used a pen and notepad.

A gentleman from our church called and asked if the deacons could come over to see me. They were going on a prayer walk on Saturday morning and thought I might like to have them come to the house and pray for me. It meant a lot to me that they sought me out. They were following the directive given in James 5:14:

> *Is anyone among you sick? Let them call the elders of the church to pray over them and anoint them with oil in the name of the Lord.*

I had previously called our pastor to make my request that the deacons pray for me. I had no idea they would come to my house.

We ended up having about twenty leaders from the church in our little living room, asking God to heal me. There was a bit of JOY shared with me that day.

During a follow-up appointment with the ENT, he examined me and thought the chemotherapy and radiation had "overcooked" me. There was a large mass of scar tissue located quite close to the carotid artery. The carotid artery supplies the brain with blood. In my case, the doctor felt it might be hazardous; it could bleed and be fatal. He recommended surgery—an oropharyngectomy, which is a procedure that is often done to remove cancer in the oropharynx, the part of the throat located at the back of the mouth. In the procedure, the doctor cuts a part of the pectoral muscle flap (in the chest) and replaces it up in the throat area to protect the carotid artery. For some patients, it may be done as part of the removal of another cancer that has spread into the oropharynx, like a large tongue cancer that has grown into the base of the tongue. We left the appointment with the doctor saying he would consult with the oncologists that were taking care of me. After discussing my case, they collectively decided to put the surgery on hold. The oncologists wanted to wait and see how my body would respond before rushing into surgery.

After a couple of weeks, I developed a red splotch around my neck. We called the ENT doctor and sent him a picture of my neck. He told us to draw a line around the splotch with a marking pen to see if the red mark would grow over the next day or so. It didn't get any larger, but the doctor thought it could be cellulitis. So he told us to head to the ER in the city. After another five-day stay at the hospital, I was sent home. This time, he switched the trach tube again, giving me a cuffless trach tube that came with a speaking valve. Remember, all this was happening post–radiation treatment.

During my stays at the hospital, it seemed like the nurses were overly interested in my use of the restroom. I am a very private person when it comes to bathroom habits. The first time I had to use the restroom in the hospital, I had to call for the nurse. My bed was "wired." In other words, if I got out of bed, an alarm would sound. I was considered a fall risk, and they didn't want me getting out of bed unattended. Even with my wife and daughter by my bedside, the alarm was set. So the nurse arrived, wrapped a strap around my waist, and followed me into the restroom. The strap was supposed to help keep me from falling. I did not need the strap, and I surely didn't need a nurse looking over my shoulder while I emptied my bladder. She stood there for a while until I finally said, "Look, I am not going to be able to do this until you leave me alone." She reluctantly left me on my own to take care of business. Give me medicine, poke me with needles, and check my vitals; but leave my visits to the bathroom to me. Eventually, we convinced some of the nurses to leave the alarm off during the night so I could get up to use the bathroom if needed.

On another bathroom issue, it seemed like each day, a nurse would ask, "Did you have a bowel movement today?" My initial thought was *No, and it's none of your business.* Of course, I could not say that, so I just uttered, "Nope." My response was usually followed with "When was the last time you had a bowel movement?" I didn't keep track, but when I am in an unfamiliar setting, I can go days without using the bathroom. When I shared that with one of the nurses, she responded with "Well, they won't let you out of here until you have a bowel movement." Dilemma: What if I can't go? I can't lie about it just to get out of the hospital. Alas, all was well. After about three days, I finally went to the bathroom one night and took care of business. But the nurses' overconcern for my bathroom habits always intrigued me.

So where was that JOY again? Maybe God was testing me while in the midst of my trial. I was sure my recovery was going to really take off during the summer, and I ended up getting worse. Romans 8:38–39 says,

> *For I am convinced that neither death nor life, nei-*
> *ther angels nor demons, neither the present nor the*
> *future, nor any powers, neither height nor depth, nor*
> *anything else in all creation, will be able to separate us*
> *from the love of God that is in Christ Jesus our Lord.*

I knew that God hadn't left me behind. He was with me, but my human weakness became evident again. It was hard to be positive and find or feel the JOY when I was ailing. Maybe the blessing was the love and care I received from my wife and daughter. They gave me great JOY. I did realize how fortunate I was to have such wonderful support. It was still hard. I didn't like not being in control. But maybe that is what I needed. Deuteronomy 31:8 declares,

The LORD himself goes before you and will be with you; he will never leave you nor forsake you. Do not be afraid; do not be discouraged.

How blessed I had been. A sore throat led to a tonsillectomy, which led to the discovery of throat cancer, which led to my treatment, which <u>brought me closer to God</u>.

God showed me how to find JOY in every single moment of every single day. There is JOY in waking up each day. There is JOY in seeing family members showing their love for me. There is JOY in experiencing support from friends. There is JOY in knowing that others were praying for me. There is JOY in our lives each day. We just need to be able to recognize it. Can we find JOY in cancer? ABSOLUTELY!

Strengthen the feeble hands, steady the knees that give way; say to those with fearful hearts, "Be strong, do not fear; your God will come, he will come with vengeance; with divine retribution he will come to save you." (Isaiah 35:3–4)

If we call to Him, He will answer us;
If we run to Him, He will run to us;
If we lift our hands, He will lift us up;
Come now praise his name, all you saints of God.

Sing for joy to God our strength;
Sing for joy to God our strength, our strength.
(Don Moen, "Sing for Joy")

Trach tube with speaking valve.

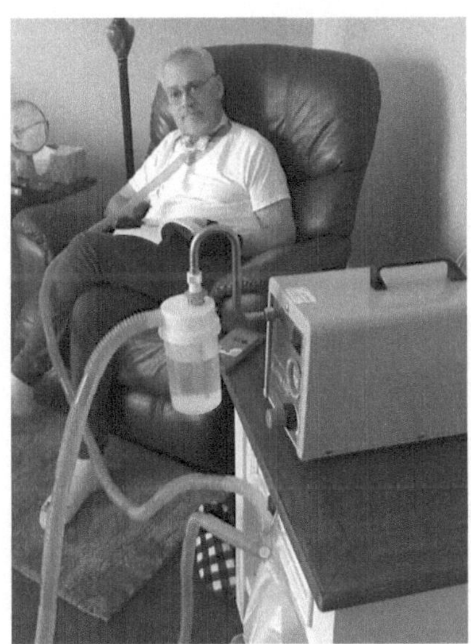

Trismus required a trach tube. I was often hooked up to machines.

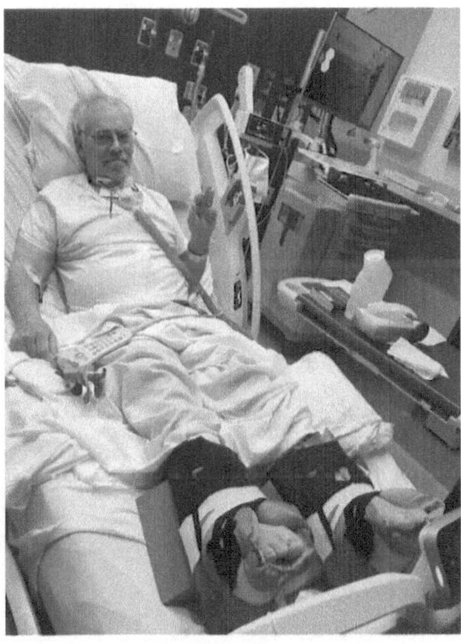

Treating issues resulting from radiation treatment.

Chapter 9

Happy Anniversary

Later in the summer, my wife and I celebrated our thirty-third wedding anniversary. I think we have a pretty good marriage, a great marriage! People always talk about marriage being hard work, but I have a different opinion. It doesn't take work if you keep the JOY of marriage in the forefront of your mind. A long time ago, I told my wife, "Thanks for marrying me." That phrase, often shortened to TFMM in texts and emails, is offered quite often. In my view, if a person thanks their life partner for choosing to be committed for a lifetime and truly means it, the marriage can be pretty smooth. So thirty-three years and counting, and we have yet to have an argument.

It pleases me to say that our kids have never heard Mom or Dad raise their voices toward each other. (They have never heard us use profanity either.) Many people don't believe it when I tell them that we have never had a fight or an argument, but it is true. We don't agree on everything, and we have our own opinions about things. But we don't argue. It is a choice. The fact that God put us together, that we choose to get along, and that we are both easygoing people has attributed to the success of our marriage. It makes me feel good to talk about it. There is a ton of JOY in our relationship.

It seems that in today's society, people get divorced so easily. There was a time when the sanctity of marriage was strong and considered a sacred bond before God. As early as the second chapter of Genesis, the first book of the Bible, the institution of marriage was established.

> The LORD God said, "It is not good for the man to be alone. I will make a helper suitable for him." (Genesis 2:18)

When God saw that there was no suitable mate for Adam, He created one.

> So the LORD God caused the man to fall into a deep sleep; and while he was sleeping, he took one of the man's ribs and then closed up the place with flesh. Then the LORD God made a woman from the rib he had taken out of the man, and he brought her to the man. The man said, "This is now bone of my bones and flesh of my flesh; she shall be called 'woman,' for she was taken out of man." That is why a man leaves his father and mother and is united to his wife, and they become one flesh. (Genesis 2:21–24)

The wife, Eve, was a gift to Adam from God, just like my wife was a gift from God to me. In my opinion, we should take special notice of the last phrase of the above passage: "and they became one flesh." That goes specifically to the value of the marriage relationship: one plus one equals one. It isn't new math. It is God's plan. In the New Testament, Mark 10:9 states,

> Therefore what God has joined together, let no one separate.

In addition, in Matthew 19:6, Jesus says,

So they are no longer two, but one flesh. Therefore, what God has joined together, let no one separate.

This is Jesus, our Savior, telling us that in marriage, the husband and wife become one entity. When we are hurting, God carries us. Maybe marriages that are hurting can also be carried by God. Maybe that idea can help keep couples together, knowing that God is carrying them when the couple struggles in their marriage.

The fifth chapter of Ephesians provides guidance for Christian households.

Submit to one another out of reverence for Christ. Wives, submit yourselves to your own husbands as you do to the Lord. For the husband is the head of the wife as Christ is the head of the church, his body, of which he is the Savior. Now as the church submits to Christ, so also wives should submit to their husbands in everything. Husbands, love your wives, just as Christ loved the church and gave himself up for her to make her holy, cleansing her by the washing with water through the word, and to present her to himself as a radiant church, without stain or wrinkle or any other blemish, but holy and blameless. In this same way, husbands ought to love their wives as their own bodies. He who loves his wife loves himself. However, each one of you also must love his wife as he loves himself, and the wife must respect her husband. (Ephesians 5:21–28, 33)

For many, this is often a bit controversial because one verse (v. 22) is often taken out of context. People do not like being submissive, but when that verse is taken within the context of the entire passage, it can be seen that there is a two-way respect for each other. It doesn't mean that one person bosses the other one around. The couple submits to each other. Mutual respect and reverence should provide a happy home. It also helps when God has His hand in the marriage!

Back to the anniversary. We didn't do much. Normally, we would go to dinner and maybe see a movie. One year, for our twenty-fifth anniversary, we took a trip to Greece and Italy—magnificent! This year, since I could not eat real food, my wife declined the invitation to go out to eat. Also, with my compromised immune system, going to the movies did not seem appropriate. We did go to physical therapy (PT). I say *we* because my wife was going to most of my appointments with me. At PT, we did tongue pulls for the first time, where the therapist literally grabbed my tongue and pulled. It was a slow, sustained pull, which was supposed to stretch the tongue. I also learned the "home alone" stretch, where my hands were placed along the jawline and gravity stretched the jaw. Our oldest son made a visit from Tulsa; he was attending a wedding and used our house as a stopover for one night. We do not get to see him enough, so it was a great celebration to have him with us even if it was for only one night.

It was time for me to get back out there and begin to experience life outside of our house. I didn't do a lot; I mostly went to church and visited on the college campus where I worked prior to retirement. Things were going pretty well. I had to get a couple of new pairs of pants and a few shirts since all my clothes were too large. My weight loss had made my wardrobe quite limited. In the midst of reclaiming regular life, I had a checkup with one of the oncologists. As it turned out, my blood work showed some low numbers again. The doctor told me to stay at home until my numbers improved. "Don't go anywhere unless you have to," she said. "And if you do go anywhere, double-mask." To me, that meant not going anywhere but doctor appointments or therapy sessions. That was a bit frustrating because there wasn't anything I could do to raise my numbers. My body had to heal itself. So it was back to the semiquarantine in our house. It took a few weeks, but my numbers climbed just enough to allow me to go out again. I still didn't do much, but at least I could go back to church.

I truly enjoy going to church and miss it when I am unable to attend. A good set of worship songs creates a mood that is conducive to listening to God speak through a pastor. I also enjoy my Sunday school class. Our class is called the Wild Bunch, and it is a great group of true friends. I would always make sure I had at least one one-dollar bill in my wallet so I could have my weekly Sunday school doughnut. (I would usually have two dollars so Keri could have a doughnut, but she is often volunteering in the nursery.) To be clear, I do not go just for the doughnut. I go for the fellowship and the learning. The doughnut is just a bonus!

Soon after I was able to go out and about again, I had a pretty good week. The occupational therapist measured the distance between my upper and lower teeth when I opened my mouth as far as I could. Up to that point, I had gone from 0.3 centimeters to 2.2 centimeters. I was recently reminded of how painful it was to yawn. In the spring and early summer, I purposefully tried not to yawn. I would catch myself and hold my jaw shut because it hurt so much when I yawned. When I wasn't thinking about it, the yawn would just appear, and I would receive a jolt of pain through my jaw. Fortunately, today, I can yawn and feel no pain.

The speech-language pathologist said I was progressing nicely; my swallowing was getting a bit better. I was going through a water protocol twice a day, where I brushed my teeth, rinsed my mouth with a salt-and-baking-soda mixture, and then took five sips of water (one half of a teaspoon each time) and practiced my swallows—three swallows per sip. There were times when I would swallow, and the water would go down the wrong tube. It was uncomfortable, but the body can handle such small amounts of water in the lungs. So there was no real threat of aspiration. Also, this week, the ENT was quite pleased with my progress; the ulcer in the back of my throat was healing from inside out. He claimed that the surgery he previously suggested might not be necessary after all. He also provided a plan for the removal of the trach tube. It might take months, but at least we had a plan.

The occupational therapist, physical therapist, and speech-language pathologist all gave me exercises to perform at home. My daughter created a chart on a whiteboard to keep me on track regarding the completion of the exercises throughout the day. It was clear that I was responsible for my own recovery. Being responsible for one's own recovery can be either intimidating or empowering. I looked at my recovery like a coach looks at training athletes. Train, train, train. Stay with it, be committed, be patient, and results would occur.

The following week, I met with my pulmonologist. He ordered a percussion vest for me to include in my daily routine. About a week later, a representative came to our house and taught us how to use the vest. The vest shakes people. There are three stages to each shake session: percussion, vibration, and drainage. Each stage lasts ten minutes. During stage 1, the vest vibrates for about two seconds and then stops, vibrates and stops, and vibrates and stops. This goes on for ten minutes. In stage 2, the vest constantly vibrates for the entire ten minutes. During stage 3, the vibrations occur in four sections of the vest, one section at a time. The overall purpose of the percussion vest is to break up the mucous collecting in the lungs. It is supposed to be a preventive measure against pneumonia. There are three settings on the vest: low, medium, and high. I always have the vest turned on high because the heavy shaking feels so good. (My wife tried the vest once; she didn't like it one bit.)

One Monday, my wife and I went to my monthly gamma globulin infusion. It was a typical infusion day—arrive, sit in a chair, get poked with needles, and sit for three and a half to four hours while the super juice flows into my body. However, in the middle of the infusion, the nurse came in to talk with us. She said, "The office is closing this Friday. You will need to arrange for a new avenue to receive your infusions." Apparently, that portion of the infectious disease office was relocating. It took a number of weeks, but we were able to arrange for me to receive the infusions at the local hospital in our town. It took a while to make all the arrangements—obtaining orders from the doctor, getting approval from Medicare since there was a change in medicine, getting reapproved once a change was made to the original orders, and scheduling my first appointment.

My infusions normally occur every four weeks, but the changeover to the new infusion center at the hospital took longer than we would have liked. So my infusion date came and went. I began to drag a bit. I could feel an increase in fatigue with each day that passed beyond my infusion date. I was a bit fearful because of my immunodeficiency. The thought of getting a cold or some other ailment loomed in my mind. In a weakened state, a simple cold could create real problems. I had to remember that God was in control. He would be with me while I waited to be infused.

> *But if we hope for what we do not yet have, we wait*
> *for it patiently.* (Romans 8:25)

Patience is not one of my strong points. Another fault of mine is that I can be overly judgmental. Sometimes, when I am judgmental, I tend to complain and criticize too much, especially when watching football games on the television. This reminds me of a quote by Coach John Wooden:

> *Let me give so much time to the improvement of*
> *myself that I shall have no time to criticize others.*

I did not like the fact that we were only given four days prior to the infectious disease office closing. I also did not like the fact that it was taking so long to get things arranged. Apparently, when the office closed, my infectious disease doctor also retired. We were dealing with another doctor whom I had never met. It ended up taking ten days before I could resume my infusions.

Once my infusions resumed, I felt that it would be okay to return to church—still wearing a mask, of course. I must say that when I returned to church, the outpouring of care and concern amazed me. People were cognizant of my condition and made a point not to shake my hand or hug me. Their cheerful faces and kind words were enough to lift me up. They were so nice, kind, and loving. They gave me great JOY. First Corinthians 13:2 says,

> *If I have the gift of prophecy and can fathom all*
> *mysteries and all knowledge, and if I have a faith*

*that can move mountains, but do not have love, I
am nothing.*

These people—my friends and my church family—were living out
the directive Jesus gave us.

There are many Scriptural passages that instruct us to love others. Here are just a couple of them:

This is my command: Love each other. (John 15:17)

*A new command I give you: Love one another. As I
have loved you, so you must love one another.* (John
13:34)

When people celebrate their anniversary, they usually revel in
the love that brought the two people together. Love is grand! But
there is a greater love than the love a couple can have for each other.
It is the love God lavishes on us every moment of every day. How
can we acknowledge God's love and not know JOY? Although it has
already been used in this book, there is merit to again noting what I
consider to be the greatest verse in the Bible:

*For God so loved the world that he gave his one and
only Son, that whoever believes in him shall not perish but have eternal life.* (John 3:16)

That one verse is enough to sustain me. The ultimate love was
when a perfect Jesus willingly died on a cross for my sin. That may be
the supreme gift of JOY. (Note: if a person was to read only one book
of the Bible, I suggest the Gospel of John; it is fabulous!)

*Let love and faithfulness never leave you; bind them
around your neck, write them on the tablet of your
heart. Then you will win favor and a good name in
the sight of God and man.* (Proverbs 3:3–4)

DENNIS DOCHEFF, ED.D.

I was sinking deep in sin
Far from the peaceful shore
Very deeply stained within
Sinking to rise no more
But the master of the sea
Heard my despairing cry,
From the waters lifted me
Now safe am I

Love lifted me! Love lifted me!
When nothing else could help
Love lifted me.
(James Rowe, "Love Lifted Me")

Keri and me at the *Colosseum* in Rome during
our twenty-fifth anniversary trip.

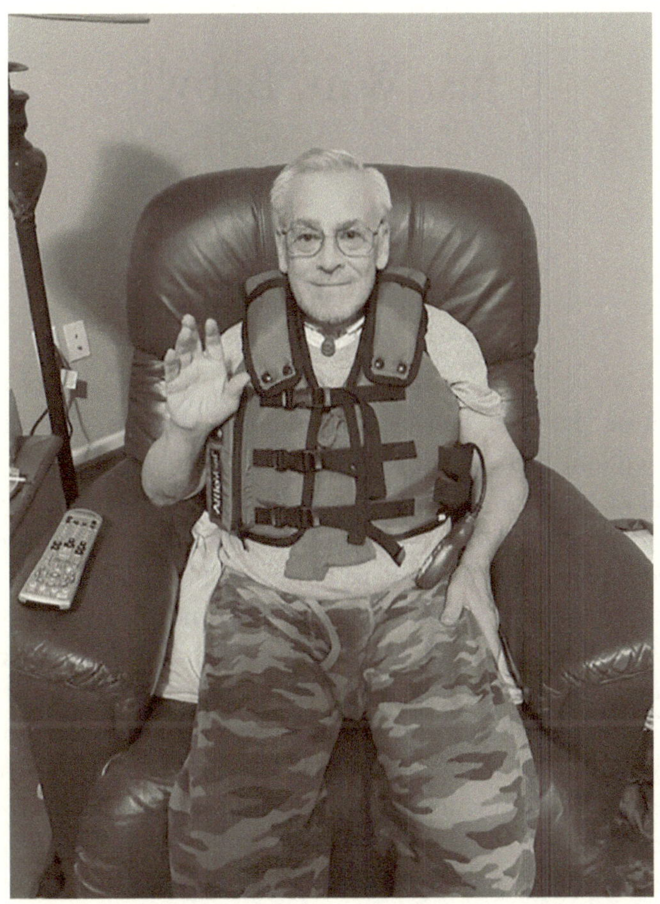

My percussion vest shakes me twice a day for thirty minutes.

Chapter 10

Just Win, Baby!

The phrase "Just win, baby" is attributed to Al Davis, a former football coach and then-owner of the Oakland Raiders of the National Football League (NFL). He is also an NFL Hall of Famer. Davis had a strong commitment to excellence; he was all about winning. He believed a player could not have a commitment to team excellence without having a personal pursuit of excellence in his own performance. Vincent T. Lombardi, another legendary NFL coach and the namesake of the Super Bowl trophy, stated, "The quality of a person's life is in direct proportion to their commitment to excellence regardless of their chosen field of endeavor." Lombardi also said, "Perfection is not attainable, but if we chase perfection, we can catch excellence."

Lombardi, one of my all-time favorite coaches, is often given credit for the quote "Winning isn't everything; it's the only thing." He later explained that he meant that the *will to win* is the only thing. Regardless, in actuality, Lombardi was not the first person to utter the quote. Back in the 1930s, UCLA Bruins football coach "Red" Sanders used this phrase in his teaching and coaching long before Lombardi. He actually took things a step further. Prior to UCLA playing its cross-town rival, USC, Sanders told his players,

"Beating SC is not a matter of life or death. It's more important than that." These sport coaches were focused on excellence and winning. Regardless of how we feel about winning a game being our main goal, the idea of playing to win is scriptural. First Corinthians 9:24 states,

> *Do you not know that in a race all the runners run,*
> *but only one receives the prize? So run that you may*
> *obtain it.*

We are called to winning. We are instructed to run our race to receive the prize. In my view, this concept can apply outside of sports. How do we go about our daily business? In our jobs, do we work to be our best? Or do we just get by? Are we the best parents we can be? Are we the best neighbors we can be? Are we winning our race?

When Herm Edwards, former NFL player and coach, said, "We play to win the game," was he indirectly including us? We must identify our game. We must define winning. We must address excellence. My game involved beating cancer. That meant that I had to have a commitment to my recovery. My excellence could be found in following orders given by the doctor, the physical therapist, the speech-language pathologist, and others who were supporting my health care. Becoming cancer-free and recovering from the chemotherapy and radiation treatments is my win. Second Timothy 4:7 says,

> *I have fought the good fight, I have finished the race,*
> *I have kept the faith.*

In my battle, my game, I must fight the good fight. I must remain faithful to God. He was with me throughout my entire treatment experience. He attended every appointment with the doctors, He felt my pain when medicine could not keep it from me, and He held my hand during sleepless nights. God always wins. I just needed to cling on to Him and find JOY in His presence. (I still do.)

There are times when life is so difficult that we want to give up. When failure slaps us in the face, we sometimes want to crawl in a hole and never come out. Theodore Roosevelt said,

> *It is not the critic who counts; not the man who points out how the strong man stumbles, or where the doer of deeds could have done them better. The credit belongs to the man who is actually in the arena, whose face is marred by dust and sweat and blood; who strives valiantly…who at best knows in the end the triumph of high achievement, and who at worst, if he fails, at least fails while daring greatly.*

Mr. Roosevelt inspired me. I wanted to be one that fought the fight. Maybe treatment and recovery shouldn't be easy; that way, we appreciate it more. It always comes back to facing adversity, standing up to our fears, and not giving up, relying on God to help us push forward regardless of our failures, fears, and circumstances. One of the greatest examples of overcoming failure and adversity can be found in the life struggle of Abraham Lincoln. Look at the timeline of his road to the presidency of the United States.

- 1816: His family was forced out of their home. He worked to support them.
- 1818: His mother died.
- 1831: He failed in business.
- 1832: He ran for state legislature—and lost.
- 1832: He also lost his job and wanted to go to law school but couldn't get in.
- 1883: He failed in business.
- 1834: He was elected to state legislature.
- 1835: His sweetheart (Ann Rutledge) died.
- 1836: He had a nervous breakdown.
- 1838: He was defeated for Speaker of the House.
- 1843: He was defeated for a nomination for Congress.
- 1846: He was elected into Congress.

- 1848: He lost a renomination into Congress.
- 1849: He was rejected for the position of land officer.
- 1854: He was defeated for the US Senate.
- 1856: He was defeated for nomination for vice president.
- 1858: He was again defeated for the US Senate.
- 1860: He was elected president of the United States.

Abraham Lincoln is a super example of perseverance—of a person facing adversity and not giving in to fear. But there have been so many others that have made it in spite of negative circumstances. Michael Jordan was cut from his high school basketball team, yet he became what some argue to be the greatest basketball player ever. Colonel Sanders couldn't sell his chicken; his recipe was rejected by over one thousand restaurants before one accepted it, and now people eat at Kentucky Fried Chicken restaurants all over the world. Viktor Frankl was a Nazi concentration camp Holocaust survivor who wrote the best-selling book *Man's Search for Meaning*. He published thirty-nine books. The Beatles were rejected by Decca Recording Studios, who said, "We don't like their sound—they have no future in show business." Yet the Beatles became the greatest rock band of all time. JK Rowling's *Harry Potter* was rejected by twelve publishers. The seven-book series has sold over 500 million copies.

The list goes on and on:

1. **Walt Disney**. His formal education ended in the eighth grade, and he was once fired from a newspaper because he lacked imagination and didn't have any original ideas. Yet he gave us Mickey Mouse and the entire Disneyland/Disney World experience, let alone the movies produced that gave us hours and hours of happiness. He stated, "All the adversity I've had in my life, all my troubles and obstacles, have strengthened me… You may not realize it when it happens, but a kick in the teeth may be the best thing in the world for you."

2. **Albert Einstein**. He struggled with language difficulties, leading some people to suggest he might have had dyslexia,

and he didn't speak fluently until he was almost six years old. Yet Einstein is recognized as one of the greatest and most influential physicists of all time. Albert Einstein is best known for developing the theory of relativity, transforming our understanding of space, time, gravity, and the universe.

3. **Wilma Rudolph**. She had many illnesses during her early childhood, including pneumonia and scarlet fever, and she contracted polio at the age of five. Because of the polio, Wilma lost strength in her left leg and foot, requiring her to wear a brace until the age of twelve. Yet Wilma Rudolph won the gold medal for the 100-meter dash, the 200-meter dash, and the 4 × 100-meter relay in the 1960 Olympics in Rome.

4. **Thomas Edison**. A sickly child, Thomas began school later than normal. Eventually, Thomas was homeschooled by his mother. Thomas developed hearing problems at the age of twelve, eventually becoming completely deaf in one ear and barely hearing in the other. He was fired from his first two jobs for being "unproductive." Yet he became one of the great inventors in history. He had over one thousand patents under his name, including the phonograph, the motion-picture camera, and the electric light bulb. It was once reported that after being asked about the ten thousand failed attempts at creating the light bulb, Edison said, "I have not *failed*. I've just found *10,000* ways that won't work."

5. **Helen Keller**. At the age of nineteen months, Helen became ill, leaving her both deaf and blind. Some doctors believe she could have had meningitis, while others think she might have had scarlet fever. Regardless, Helen Keller could not see or hear, yet she learned to communicate and "feel" music. In 1904, Keller graduated from Radcliffe College, becoming the first deaf-blind person to earn a bachelor of arts degree. Keller was a world-famous speaker and an author of twelve books. She was a strong advocate for people with disabilities.

Each one of these famous people faced adversity in their lives. They can be inspiring to many of us, yet I am greatly inspired by young people who overcome obstacles. When I see television commercials for St. Jude Children's Research Hospital, I am floored by the resiliency of those children. Kids have such big hearts. They do not give up! Jim Valvano, a former NCAA basketball coach who lost his battle with cancer, gave us a now-famous seven-word line:

Don't give up... Don't ever give up.

He also said,

Cancer can take away my physical abilities. It cannot touch my mind, it cannot touch my heart, and it cannot touch my soul.

His battle with cancer was quite visible to the public. Coach Valvano, along with ESPN, founded the *V Foundation for Cancer Research*, which has raised millions of dollars for cancer research. His quotes should be inspirational to all; they were for me.

I was teaching and coaching at a small school, and we had an interim principal for one year. Since he was a longtime coach and athletic director, I quickly developed a good relationship with him. Allow me to share a story about a high school student-athlete that was shared by this older, experienced educator. He was once tasked to help build a new school offering the latest in teaching methods and learning theory. Because he wanted to infiltrate the entire school and influence as many kids as possible, he made a point to attend as many extracurricular events as possible. This included sporting events as well as theater productions and music concerts. He was always a fan of the big sports: football, basketball, and baseball.

One day, his school was hosting a cross country meet that included a number of schools. This principal never really cared much for cross country. He didn't like to run distance and was never a real supporter of the sport. But in this case, he made a point to attend the meet so he could support the student-athletes and also be seen there by students and parents. Because his schedule was so tight, he was running a bit late. The race was run on a course that wound around some fields on campus and then through a wooded area next to the track. The runners would then come out of the woods and make one lap around the track to finish the race. As he walked down to the track, he noticed that some runners had already completed the course.

He continued his walk to the track, seeing that some runners and their parents were actually leaving the facility. They were done. But there was one school that had all of its runners and many parents stay behind. The kids on that cross country team began to line the track, standing a certain distance apart so that they could circle the entire running oval. All of a sudden, the principal heard a student holler, "Here she comes!" The students and parents who remained behind all began to scream and cheer. Off in the distance, the principal saw a tiny head appear. This young girl was chugging along at a very slow pace. *She must be the last one,* he thought. He debated whether to stay or leave. He decided he better stay; he didn't want people to see him leave with only one runner left in the race.

So as the young girl came over a rise, the principal could see almost all of the girl. To say her running style was awkward would have been an understatement. But the cheering continued, getting louder as the girl approached the track. *What is going on here?* thought the principal. He walked down closer to the track where he could get a better look at the girl. Literally everyone left behind was cheering. As the principal got a little closer to the finish line, he noticed that this short, clumsy-looking girl had no feet—none. She was running on stumps. He stood there, frozen, mouth agape. The girl was surrounded by teammates and parents as she finished the race. She finished! She won! She was a champion!

As the sporting event concluded, the last team headed for the parking lot to get on the bus and travel home. The principal watched as the diminutive girl walked by, enveloped among her fans (teammates and parents). She walked a bit "funny," quite awkward. But as a tear began to run down the principal's cheek, he saw the JOY in her face, the sweetness of her smile, and the gleam in her eyes; and he was changed forever.

We do not need to use famous people as our heroes, people we look up to. There are people all around us who can provide inspiration with their stories of overcoming adversity, facing their fears, and becoming successful. They found their "yet." Here is a poem about "yet" that was sent to me via Facebook (author unknown).

The Power of Yet

"I don't get it."
"I can't do this."
"This doesn't work."
Take a deep breath. Go for a short stroll.
Then add a "yet" to the end of your sentence.
"I don't get it…yet."
"I can't do this…yet."
"This doesn't work…yet."
It may not be easy, but it doesn't mean
you're never going to meet the challenge.

We can use *yet* to ensure a more positive mindset as we face challenges, trials, and adversity of all kinds. Another way to use *yet* is to take a negative statement and turn it into a positive declaration—for example, "I don't like cleaning up after the kids, yet it gives me pleasure to care for them," "I really don't care for my job, yet it does provide my family with a home and food on the table," and "I haven't completed my recovery from cancer, yet I have confidence in myself and trust my Lord to carry me to the finish line."

We can determine our success. Recall the tiny elderly women ("bag of bones") who inspired me at the cancer center. Think of someone you know that has an inspiring story. Then show gratitude to them for giving you the inspiration needed to face your trials. Find your JOY!

And then there is me. Recently I received a bite expander in the mail. It was ordered by the ENT, one of the doctors caring for me. I am supposed to place this plastic contraption into my mouth, bite down on upper and lower padded areas, and squeeze the handle, which stretches my bite. There are numerous protocols to follow: seven seconds of stretching, seven seconds of rest, and repeat seven times or five seconds of stretching, five seconds of rest, and repeat thirty times. Or I can stretch and hold for five minutes, rest, and repeat. It is not something that is pleasant, but most of my caregivers told me it would be a great assist in my recovery. So I do it.

What happens now? At the time of this writing, I was still completing my recovery. Compromised immune system? Yes. Still have the feeding tube? Yes. Still have the trach in my throat? Yes. Still fatigued? Yes. Still wearing braces on my legs? Yes. Still shaking in my percussion vest twice a day? Yes. Still coughing up loads of goo? Yes. Yet I have great JOY knowing that Jesus has gone to heaven to prepare a place for me to live in eternity. I have great JOY being an heir, adopted into the family of God. I have great JOY in feeling content regardless of my situation on this temporary residence we call earth. On a smaller scale, I know that someday, I will be able to swallow and eat food again; I will have a free feeling around my throat, which will not be clasped by a collar holding a trach; and I will be able to exercise again. By the way, the last CT scan and PET scan showed no cancer. Just win, baby! I found JOY in cancer!

The Chinese philosopher Lao Tzu said,

The journey of a thousand miles begins with one step.

Robert Lloyd said,

Slow and steady wins the race.

Because of the LORD's great love we are not consumed, for his compassions never fail. They are new every morning; great is your faithfulness. (Lamentations 3:23)

Pardon for sin and a peace that endureth,
Thine own dear presence to cheer and to guide,
Strength for today and bright hope for tomorrow—
Blessings all mine with ten thousand beside!

Great is Thy faithfulness!
Great is Thy faithfulness!
Morning by morning new mercies I see;
All I have needed Thy hand hath provided—
Great is Thy faithfulness, Lord, unto me.
(Thomas Chisholm "Great Is Thy Faithfulness")

Bite expander helping me to open up my mouth.

"Feeding" four times a day. Someday I will have a cheeseburger!

Afterword

This story does not end. It does not end because the author is still living and enjoying each day. As stated earlier in the book, "Make each day your masterpiece." Although I am still working through the aftereffects of my chemotherapy and radiation treatment and recovery from throat cancer, I try to find JOY in each day, even on those days when I don't feel very well. The bottom line is that I have to learn to be content. It is definitely a learning process, as the apostle Paul indicated in Philippians 4:11–13:

> *I am not saying this because I am in need, for I have learned to be content whatever the circumstances. I know what it is to be in need, and I know what it is to have plenty. I have learned the secret of being content in any and every situation, whether well fed or hungry, whether living in plenty or in want. I can do all this through him who gives me strength.*

My being content does not depend upon my circumstances. Being content comes from within: knowing God is with me, protecting me and loving me no matter what! I am not sure a person can find true JOY without some element of contentedness. Even when things do not go my way, I can be content. I can feel JOY. True, pure, and eternal JOY is not something we create. It is a gift from God, waiting for us to reach out and grasp it. I now have different goals in my life.

- Goal 1: Live in obedience to Jesus Christ. He has given me eternal life. I owe everything to Him. He lives in me not because of anything I have done. I did not earn it. I am forever indebted to Him because of His love, grace, and mercy. Find JOY.
- Goal 2: Love my wife and children every day and not just love them but also demonstrate that love. If I live in a manner where I am driven to be an optimistic leader, an encourager, and a positive role model, each one of them should benefit. I pray each of them will experience JOY.
- Goal 3: Be kind to others. A long time ago, President George H. W. Bush called our nation to be a "kinder, gentler nation." That is what we need in our society today, and it begins with me. I need to share my JOY with others.
- Goal 4: Be content. Do not let my circumstances dictate how I perceive life. Be still and know that He is God. Always praise Him in all situations, finding JOY in all that life brings.

*For I am not ashamed of the gospel, because it is
the power of God that brings salvation to everyone
who believes: first to the Jew, then to the Gentile.*
(Romans 1:16)

*I heard an old, old story
How a Savior came from glory
How He gave His life on Calvary
To save a wretch like me
I heard about His groaning
Of His precious blood's atoning
Then I repented of my sins
And won the victory.*

O victory in Jesus
My Savior forever;
He sought me and bought me
With His redeeming blood;
He loved me 'ere I knew Him
And all my love is due Him;
He plunged me to victory
Beneath the cleansing flood.
(Eugene Monroe Bartlett, "Victory in Jesus")

I want to leave the reader with a poem titled "The Dash" by Linda Ellis. Once the poem is read, readers are encouraged to consider their own personal dash, then live in a fashion that expands that dash by being a positive member of society.

I read of a man who stood to speak
at the funeral of a friend.
He referred to the dates on the tombstone,
from the beginning…to the end.
He noted that first came the date of birth
and spoke the following date with tears,
But he said what mattered most of all
was the dash between those years.
For that dash represents all the time
that they spent alive on earth.
And now only those who loved them
know what that little line is worth.
For it matters not, how much we own,
the cars…the house…the cash.
What matters is how we live and love
and how we spend our dash.
So, think about this long and hard, are
there things you'd like to change?
For you never know how much time is
left that can still be rearranged.

DENNIS DOCHEFF, ED.D.

If we could just slow down enough to
consider what's true and real.
And always try to understand
the way other people feel.
And be less quick to anger, and
show appreciation more.
And love the people in our lives
like we've never loved before.
If we treat each other with respect
and more often wear a smile,
Remembering this special dash
might only last a little while.
So, when your eulogy is being read,
with your life's actions to rehash…
Would you be proud of the things they say
about how you spent YOUR dash?

Christmas 2022 (Left to right: Dodge, Payton,
Andrea [holding Keeley], Emily and RJ)!

One happy grandpa!

Closing Prayer

Lord, thank You for the JOY offered to us in each moment You provide. Thank You for the opportunity to create this book and share my story. It is my hope that others might seek JOY during their trials in life. Lord, if only one reader finds greater inner strength, realizing it was because of Your presence, then the effort required to create this little book was worth it. Please allow others to find JOY during troubled times. Let this story please You, providing others with the gospel message: Jesus Christ died on the cross, washed away our sins, and rose on the third day. In Your Son's name I pray. Amen.

> *[F]or all have sinned and fall short of the glory of God, and all are justified freely by his grace through the redemption that came by Christ Jesus. God presented Christ as a sacrifice of atonement, through the shedding of his blood—to be received by faith. He did this to demonstrate his righteousness, because in his forbearance he had left the sins committed beforehand unpunished—he did it to demonstrate his righteousness at the present time, so as to be just and the one who justifies those who have faith in Jesus.* (Romans 3:23–26)

But God demonstrates his own love for us in this: While we were still sinners, Christ died for us. (Romans 5:8)

Get rid of all bitterness, rage and anger, brawling and slander, along with every form of malice. Be kind and compassionate to one another, forgiving each other, just as in Christ God forgave you. (Ephesians 4:31–32)

Bible Verses Used in the Book

All scripture passages included in this book are in the New International Version (NIV). I am clearly not a biblical scholar, but the verses used are those that are meaningful to me based upon my understanding and interpretation of God's Word. Readers are encouraged to scour the Bible and determine the truthfulness, power, and JOY found in God's Word for themselves.

These passages were selected for inclusion in this book for two reasons: 1) some of the verses are included because they are my favorites, and 2) it seemed appropriate to insert God's Word throughout the book. It is such an important part of my life that I could not separate the Bible, God's Word, from my story.

Verses (listed alphabetically)

- 1 Corinthians 1:9, "God is faithful, who has called you into fellowship with his Son, Jesus Christ our Lord."
- 1 Corinthians 9:24, "Do you not know that in a race all the runners run, but only one receives the prize? So run that you may obtain it."
- 1 Corinthians 10:13, "No temptation has overtaken you except what is common to mankind. And God is faithful; he will not let you be tempted beyond what you can bear.

But when you are tempted, he will also provide a way out so that you can endure it."

- 1 Corinthians 11:1, "Follow my example, as I follow the example of Christ."
- 1 Corinthians 13:2, "If I have the gift of prophecy and can fathom all mysteries and all knowledge, and if I have a faith that can move mountains, but do not have love, I am nothing."
- 1 Corinthians 13:4–5, "Love is patient, love is kind. It does not envy, it does not boast, it is not proud. It does not dishonor others, it is not self-seeking, it is not easily angered, it keeps no record of wrongs."
- 1 John 3:18, "Dear children, let us not love with words or speech but with actions and in truth."
- 1 Peter 1:6, "In this you greatly rejoice, even though now for a little while, if necessary, you have been distressed by various trials."
- 1 Peter 1:8–9, "[A]nd though you have not seen Him, you love Him, and though you do not see Him now, but believe in Him, you greatly rejoice with joy inexpressible and full of glory, obtaining as the outcome of your faith the salvation of your souls."
- 1 Peter 2:12, "Live such good lives among the pagans that, though they accuse you of doing wrong, they may see your good deeds and glorify God on the day he visits us."
- 1 Peter 4:19, "So then, those who suffer according to God's will should commit themselves to their faithful Creator and continue to do good."
- 1 Samuel 17:45, 47, "David said to the Philistine, 'You come against me with sword and spear and javelin, but I come against you in the name of the Lord Almighty, the God of the armies of Israel, whom you have defied. All those gathered here will know that it is not by sword or spear that the LORD saves; for the battle is the LORD's, and he will give all of you into our hands.'"

- 2 Corinthians 1:3–4, "Blessed be the God and Father of our Lord Jesus Christ, the Father of mercies and God of all comfort, who comforts us in all our affliction so that we will be able to comfort those who are in any affliction with the comfort with which we ourselves are comforted by God."
- 2 Corinthians 4:17–18, "For our light and momentary troubles are achieving for us an eternal glory that far out-weighs them all. So we fix our eyes not on what is seen, but on what is unseen, since what is seen is temporary, but what is unseen is eternal."
- 2 Corinthians 9:8, "And God is able to bless you abundantly, so that in all things at all times, having all that you need, you will abound in every good work."
- 2 Corinthians 12:9–10, "But he said to me, 'My grace is sufficient for you, for my power is made perfect in weakness.' Therefore I will boast all the more gladly about my weaknesses, so that Christ's power may rest on me. That is why, for Christ's sake, I delight in weaknesses, in insults, in hardships, in persecutions, in difficulties. For when I am weak, then I am strong."
- 2 Peter 3:9, "The Lord is not slow in keeping his promise, as some understand slowness. Instead he is patient with you, not wanting anyone to perish, but everyone to come to repentance."
- 2 Thessalonians 3:3, "But the Lord is faithful, and he will strengthen you and protect you from the evil one."
- 2 Timothy 4:7, "I have fought the good fight, I have finished the race, I have kept the faith."
- Colossians 3:12, "Therefore, as God's chosen people, holy and dearly loved, clothe yourselves with compassion, kindness, humility, gentleness and patience."
- Deuteronomy 31:8, "The Lord himself goes before you and will be with you; he will never leave you nor forsake you. Do not be afraid; do not be discouraged."

- Ephesians 2:8–9, "For it is by grace you have been saved, through faith—and this is not from yourselves, it is the gift of God—not by works, so that no one can boast."
- Ephesians 2:10, "For we are God's handiwork, created in Christ Jesus to do good works, which God prepared in advance for us to do."
- Ephesians 4:31–32, "Get rid of all bitterness, rage and anger, brawling and slander, along with every form of malice. Be kind and compassionate to one another, forgiving each other, just as in Christ God forgave you."
- Ephesians 5:21–28, 33, "Submit to one another out of reverence for Christ. Wives, submit yourselves to your own husbands as you do to the Lord. For the husband is the head of the wife as Christ is the head of the church, his body, of which he is the Savior. Now as the church submits to Christ, so also wives should submit to their husbands in everything. Husbands, love your wives, just as Christ loved the church and gave himself up for her to make her holy, cleansing her by the washing with water through the word, and to present her to himself as a radiant church, without stain or wrinkle or any other blemish, but holy and blameless. In this same way, husbands ought to love their wives as their own bodies. He who loves his wife loves himself. However, each one of you also must love his wife as he loves himself, and the wife must respect her husband."
- Ephesians 6:12, "For our struggle is not against flesh and blood, but against the rulers, against the authorities, against the powers of this dark world and against the spiritual forces of evil in the heavenly realms."
- Exodus 33:14, "The Lord replied, 'My Presence will go with you, and I will give you rest.'"
- Galatians 5:22–23, "But the fruit of the Spirit is love, joy, peace, forbearance, kindness, goodness, faithfulness, gentleness and self-control. Against such things there is no law."

- Galatians 6:9, "Let us not become weary in doing good, for at the proper time we will reap a harvest if we do not give up."
- Genesis 2:18, "The Lord God said, "It is not good for the man to be alone. I will make a helper suitable for him."
- Hebrews 10:22, "Let us draw near to God with a sincere heart and with the full assurance that faith brings, having our hearts sprinkled to cleanse us from a guilty conscience and having our bodies washed with pure water."
- Hebrews 12:1–2, "Therefore, since we are surrounded by such a great cloud of witnesses, let us throw off everything that hinders and the sin that so easily entangles. And let us run with perseverance the race marked out for us, fixing our eyes on Jesus, the pioneer and perfecter of faith. For the joy set before him he endured the cross, scorning its shame, and sat down at the right hand of the throne of God."
- Hebrews 12:1–3, "Therefore, since we are surrounded by such a great cloud of witnesses, let us throw off everything that hinders and the sin that so easily entangles. And let us run with perseverance the race marked out for us, fixing our eyes on Jesus, the pioneer and perfecter of faith. For the joy set before him he endured the cross, scorning its shame, and sat down at the right hand of the throne of God. Consider him who endured such opposition from sinners, so that you will not grow weary and lose heart."
- Hebrews 13:5, "Keep your lives free from the love of money and be content with what you have, because God has said, 'Never will I leave you; never will I forsake you.'"
- Isaiah 35:3–4, "Strengthen the feeble hands, steady the knees that give way; say to those with fearful hearts, 'Be strong, do not fear; your God will come, he will come with vengeance; with divine retribution he will come to save you.'"
- Isaiah 41:10, "So do not fear, for I am with you; do not be dismayed, for I am your God. I will strengthen you and help you; I will uphold you with my righteous right hand."

- Isaiah 41:13, "For I am the LORD your God who takes hold of your right hand and says to you, Do not fear; I will help you."
- Isaiah 43:2, "When you pass through the waters, I will be with you; And through the rivers, they will not overflow you. When you walk through the fire, you will not be scorched, Nor will the flame burn you."
- James 1:2–3, "Consider it pure joy, my brothers and sisters, whenever you face trials of many kinds, because you know that the testing of your faith produces perseverance."
- James 1:12, "Blessed is the one who perseveres under trial because, having stood the test, that person will receive the crown of life that the Lord has promised to those who love him."
- James 1:19–20, "My dear brothers and sisters, take note of this: Everyone should be quick to listen, slow to speak and slow to become angry, because human anger does not produce the righteousness that God desires."
- James 4:8, 10, "Come near to God and he will come near to you. Wash your hands, you sinners, and purify your hearts, you double-minded. Humble yourselves before the Lord, and he will lift you up."
- James 5:14, "Is anyone among you sick? Let them call the elders of the church to pray over them and anoint them with oil in the name of the Lord."
- Jeremiah 29:11, "'For I know the plans I have for you,' declares the Lord, 'plans to prosper you and not to harm you, plans to give you hope and a future.'"
- John 3:16, 18, "For God so loved the world that he gave his one and only Son, that whoever believes in him shall not perish but have eternal life. Whoever believes in him is not condemned, but whoever does not believe stands condemned already because they have not believed in the name of God's one and only Son."

- John 6:2, "[A]nd a great crowd of people followed him because they saw the signs he had performed by healing the sick."
- John 13:34, "A new command I give you: Love one another. As I have loved you, so you must love one another."
- John 14:27, "Peace I leave with you; my peace I give you. I do not give to you as the world gives. Do not let your hearts be troubled and do not be afraid."
- John 15:5, "I am the vine; you are the branches. If you remain in me and I in you, you will bear much fruit; apart from me you can do nothing."
- John 15:10–13, "If you keep my commands, you will remain in my love, just as I have kept my Father's commands and remain in his love. I have told you this so that my joy may be in you and that your joy may be complete. My command is this: Love each other as I have loved you. Greater love has no one than this: to lay down one's life for one's friends."
- John 15:17, "This is my command: Love each other."
- John 16:33, "I have told you these things, so that in me you may have peace. In this world you will have trouble. But take heart! I have overcome the world."
- Joshua 1:6–7, 9, "Be strong and courageous, because you will lead these people to inherit the land I swore to their ancestors to give them. 'Be strong and very courageous. Be careful to obey all the law my servant Moses gave you; do not turn from it to the right or to the left, that you may be successful wherever you go. Have I not commanded you? Be strong and courageous. Do not be afraid; do not be discouraged, for the Lord your God will be with you wherever you go.'"
- Lamentations 3:22–23, "Because of the Lord's great love we are not consumed, for his compassions never fail. They are new every morning; great is your faithfulness."
- Luke 1:30–33, "But the angel said to her, 'Do not be afraid, Mary; you have found favor with God. You will conceive

and give birth to a son, and you are to call him Jesus. He will be great and will be called the Son of the Most High. The Lord God will give him the throne of his father David, and he will reign over Jacob's descendants forever; his kingdom will never end.'"

- Luke 6: 31–35, "Do to others as you would have them do to you. 'If you love those who love you, what credit is that to you? Even sinners love those who love them. And if you do good to those who are good to you, what credit is that to you? Even sinners do that. And if you lend to those from whom you expect repayment, what credit is that to you? Even sinners lend to sinners, expecting to be repaid in full. But love your enemies, do good to them, and lend to them without expecting to get anything back. Then your reward will be great, and you will be children of the Most High, because he is kind to the ungrateful and wicked.'"

- Luke 12:24, "Consider the ravens: They do not sow or reap, they have no storeroom or barn; yet God feeds them. And how much more valuable you are than birds!"

- Mark 2:17, "On hearing this, Jesus said to them, 'It is not the healthy who need a doctor, but the sick. I have not come to call the righteous, but sinners.'"

- Mark 5:25–29, 33–34, "And a woman was there who had been subject to bleeding for twelve years. She had suffered a great deal under the care of many doctors and had spent all she had, yet instead of getting better she grew worse. When she heard about Jesus, she came up behind him in the crowd and touched his cloak, because she thought, 'If I just touch his clothes, I will be healed.' Immediately her bleeding stopped and she felt in her body that she was freed from her suffering. Then the woman, knowing what had happened to her, came and fell at his feet and, trembling with fear, told him the whole truth. He said to her, 'Daughter, your faith has healed you. Go in peace and be freed from your suffering.'"

- Mark 10:9, "Therefore what God has joined together, let no one separate."
- Matthew 5:16, "In the same way, let your light shine before others, that they may see your good deeds and glorify your Father in heaven."
- Matthew 6:8, "Do not be like them, for your Father knows what you need before you ask him."
- Matthew 6:9–13, "This, then, is how you should pray: 'Our Father in heaven, hallowed be your name, your kingdom come, your will be done, on earth as it is in heaven. Give us today our daily bread. And forgive us our debts, as we also have forgiven our debtors. And lead us not into temptation, but deliver us from the evil one.'"
- Matthew 7:11, "If you, then, though you are evil, know how to give good gifts to your children, how much more will your Father in heaven give good gifts to those who ask him!"
- Matthew 11:28, "Come to me, all you who are weary and burdened, and I will give you rest."
- Matthew 14:27–29, "But Jesus immediately said to them: 'Take courage! It is I. Don't be afraid.' 'Lord, if it's you,' Peter replied, 'tell me to come to you on the water.' 'Come,' he said. Then Peter got down out of the boat, walked on the water and came toward Jesus."
- Matthew 19:6, "So they are no longer two, but one flesh. Therefore what God has joined together, let no one separate."
- Matthew 19:14, "Jesus said, 'Let the little children come to me, and do not hinder them, for the kingdom of heaven belongs to such as these.'"
- Matthew 28:19–20, "Therefore go and make disciples of all nations, baptizing them in the name of the Father and of the Son and of the Holy Spirit, and teaching them to obey everything I have commanded you. And surely I am with you always, to the very end of the age."

- Philippians 2:3–4, "Do nothing out of selfish ambition or vain conceit. Rather, in humility value others above yourselves, not looking to your own interests but each of you to the interests of the others."
- Philippians 3:13–14, "Brothers and sisters, I do not consider myself yet to have taken hold of it. But one thing I do: Forgetting what is behind and straining toward what is ahead, I press on toward the goal to win the prize for which God has called me heavenward in Christ Jesus."
- Philippians 4:6–7, "Do not be anxious about anything, but in every situation, by prayer and petition, with thanksgiving, present your requests to God. And the peace of God, which transcends all understanding, will guard your hearts and your minds in Christ Jesus."
- Philippians 4:8, "Finally, brothers and sisters, whatever is true, whatever is noble, whatever is right, whatever is pure, whatever is lovely, whatever is admirable—if anything is excellent or praiseworthy—think about such things."
- Philippians 4:11–13, "I am not saying this because I am in need, for I have learned to be content whatever the circumstances. I know what it is to be in need, and I know what it is to have plenty. I have learned the secret of being content in any and every situation, whether well fed or hungry, whether living in plenty or in want. I can do all this through him who gives me strength."
- Philippians 4:19, "And my God will meet all your needs according to the riches of his glory in Christ Jesus."
- Proverbs 3:3–4, "Let love and faithfulness never leave you; bind them around your neck, write them on the tablet of your heart. Then you will win favor and a good name in the sight of God and man."
- Proverbs 3:5–6, "Trust in the LORD with all your heart and lean not on your own understanding; in all your ways submit to him, and he will make your paths straight."

- Proverbs 4:25–26, "Let your eyes look straight ahead; fix your gaze directly before you. Give careful thought to the paths for your feet and be steadfast in all your ways."
- Psalm 28:7, "The Lord is my strength and my shield; My heart trusts in Him, and I am helped; Therefore my heart exults, And with my song I shall thank Him."
- Psalm 40:2, "He lifted me out of the slimy pit, out of the mud and mire; he set my feet on a rock and gave me a firm place to stand."
- Psalm 42:5, "Why, my soul, are you downcast? Why so disturbed within me? Put your hope in God, for I will yet praise him, my Savior and my God."
- Psalm 46:1–3, "God is our refuge and strength, a very present help in trouble. Therefore we will not fear, though the earth should change and though the mountains slip into the heart of the sea; Though its waters roar and foam, though the mountains quake at its swelling pride."
- Psalm 46:1–11, "God is our refuge and strength, an ever-present help in trouble. Therefore we will not fear, though the earth give way and the mountains fall into the heart of the sea, though its waters roar and foam and the mountains quake with their surging. There is a river whose streams make glad the city of God, the holy place where the Most High dwells. God is within her, she will not fall; God will help her at break of day. Nations are in uproar, kingdoms fall; he lifts his voice, the earth melts. The Lord Almighty is with us; the God of Jacob is our fortress. Come and see what the Lord has done, the desolations he has brought on the earth. He makes wars cease to the ends of the earth. He breaks the bow and shatters the spear; he burns the shields with fire. He says, 'Be still, and know that I am God; I will be exalted among the nations, I will be exalted in the earth.' The Lord Almighty is with us; the God of Jacob is our fortress."
- Psalm 48:14, "For this God is our God for ever and ever; he will be our guide even to the end."

- Psalm 117:2, "For great is his love toward us, and the faithfulness of the LORD endures forever. Praise the LORD."
- Psalm 145:13, "Your kingdom is an everlasting kingdom, and your dominion endures through all generations. The Lord is trustworthy in all he promises and faithful in all he does."
- Romans 1:16, "For I am not ashamed of the gospel, because it is the power of God that brings salvation to everyone who believes: first to the Jew, then to the Gentiles."
- Romans 3:23–26, "[F]or all have sinned and fall short of the glory of God, and all are justified freely by his grace through the redemption that came by Christ Jesus. God presented Christ as a sacrifice of atonement, through the shedding of his blood—to be received by faith. He did this to demonstrate his righteousness, because in his forbearance he had left the sins committed beforehand unpunished—he did it to demonstrate his righteousness at the present time, so as to be just and the one who justifies those who have faith in Jesus."
- Romans 5:3–4, "And not only this, but we also exult in our tribulations, knowing that tribulation brings about perseverance; and perseverance, proven character; and proven character, hope."
- Romans 5:8, "But God demonstrates his own love for us in this: While we were still sinners, Christ died for us."
- Romans 8:25, "But if we hope for what we do not yet have, we wait for it patiently."
- Romans 8:28, "And we know that in all things God works for the good of those who love him, who have been called according to his purpose."
- Romans 8:35, "Who shall separate us from the love of Christ? Shall trouble or hardship or persecution or famine or nakedness or danger or sword?"
- Romans 8:38–39, "For I am convinced that neither death nor life, neither angels nor demons, neither the present nor the future, nor any powers, neither height nor depth, nor

anything else in all creation, will be able to separate us from the love of God that is in Christ Jesus our Lord."

- Romans 12:12, "Be joyful in hope, patient in affliction, faithful in prayer."
- Romans 15:13, "May the God of hope fill you with all joy and peace as you trust in him, so that you may overflow with hope by the power of the Holy Spirit."

About the Author

Dennis Docheff was in the education profession for forty-two years. His experience included teaching and coaching at the elementary, middle school, high school, and collegiate levels. Dennis also filled the roles of elementary principal, middle school athletic director, high school counselor, college professor, and department chair. Dennis's areas of expertise are focused on teaching and coaching effectiveness, curriculum, and administration.

Dennis is happily married to Keri. Keri and Dennis have three children: two sons and a daughter (Dodge, Payton, and Emily). Dennis considers his family his greatest earthly treasure.

After over fifty years of good health, Dennis survived battles with both leukemia as well as throat cancer. He considers himself blessed to have experienced difficult trials as they brought him nearer to God. God is always faithful!

Highlights in Docheff's professional career include a three-year stint at the United States Military Academy at West Point; serving as president of the National Association for Sport and Physical Education (NASPE); serving as president of the Central District Association of the American Alliance for Health, Physical Education, Recreation and Dance (AAHPERD); and serving as president for the Missouri Society of Health and Physical Education (MOSHAPE). Dennis has had over 125 articles published in professional journals, given over three hundred professional presentations, and written four other books.

Awards and recognitions he has received include the following:

- 2022 Kathleen Kinderfather Award (MOSHAPE)
- 2018 Joy of Effort Award (SHAPE America)
- 2018 Byler Distinguished Faculty Award (University of Central Missouri)
- 2015 Mark Harvey Legacy Award (SHAPE America Central District)
- 2012 Robert M. Taylor Professional Service Honor Award (MOSHAPE)
- 2011 Honor Award (SHAPE America)
- 2011 Excellence in Service Award (UCM College of Health and Human Services)
- 2005 Scholar Award (MOSHAPE)
- 1999 Commander's Award for Civilian Service (United States Military Academy at West Point)

Dennis's favorite Bible passage is Philippians 2:3–4: "Do nothing out of selfish ambition or vain conceit. Rather, in humility value others above yourselves, not looking to your own interests but each of you to the interests of the others."

www.ingramcontent.com/pod-product-compliance
Lightning Source LLC
Chambersburg PA
CBHW061343160726
47995CB00001B/149